Card Making
Handmade Greetings for All Occasions

Stylish Thanks, page 96

www.companyscoming.com
visit our website

Front Cover: Happy Birthday, page 56

Card Making

Second Printing June 2008

Library and Archives Canada Cataloguing in Publication
Card making.
Includes index.
ISBN 978-1-897069-76-9
1. Greeting cards.
T872.C37 2008   745.594'1   C2007-905521-4

Published by
Company's Coming Publishing Limited
2311-96 Street
Edmonton, Alberta, Canada T6N 1G3
Tel: 780-450-6223 Fax: 780-450-1857
www.companyscoming.com

Printed in China

THE COMPANY'S COMING STORY

Jean Paré grew up with an understanding that family, friends and home cooking are the key ingredients for a good life. A mother of four, Jean worked as a professional caterer for eighteen years, operating out of her home kitchen. During that time, she came to appreciate quick and easy recipes that call for everyday ingredients. In answer to mounting requests for her recipes, Company's Coming cookbooks were born, and Jean moved on to a new chapter in her career.

Company's Coming founder Jean Paré

In the beginning, Jean worked from a spare bedroom in her home, located in the small prairie town of Vermilion, Alberta, Canada. The first Company's Coming cookbook, 150 Delicious Squares, was an immediate bestseller. Today, with well over 100 titles in print, Company's Coming has earned the distinction of being the publisher of Canada's most popular cookbooks. The company continues to gain new supporters by adhering to Jean's 'Golden Rule of Cooking'—never share a recipe you wouldn't use yourself. It's an approach that works—millions of times over!

Company's Coming cookbooks are distributed throughout Canada, the United States, Australia and other international English-language markets. French and Spanish language editions have also been published. Sales to date have surpassed 25 million copies with no end in sight. Familiar and trusted in home kitchens around the world, Company's Coming cookbooks are highly regarded both as kitchen workbooks and as family heirlooms.

Just as Company's Coming continues to promote the tradition of home cooking, now the same is true with crafting. Like cooking, successful crafts depend upon easy-to-follow instructions, readily available materials and enticing photographs of the finished products. Also like cooking, crafts are meant to be enjoyed in the home or cottage. Company's Coming Crafts, then, seems to be a natural extension from the kitchen into the family room or den.

Because Company's Coming operates a test kitchen and not a craft shop, we've partnered with a major North American craft publisher to assemble a variety of craft compilations exclusively for us. Our editors have been involved every step of the way. You can see the results for yourself in the book you're holding.

Company's Coming Crafts are for everyone—whether you're a beginner or a seasoned pro. What better gift could you offer than something you've made yourself? In these hectic days, people still enjoy crafting parties—whether it be knitting, card making, quilting or any of a wide range of crafts. Crafting brings family and friends together in the same way that a good meal tightens the bond between family and friends. Company's Coming is proud to support crafters with this new craft book series.

We hope you enjoy these easy-to-follow, informative, colourful books and that they will inspire your creativity! So don't delay—get crafty!

CONTENTS

Between the Covers 6 • Foreword 7 • General Instructions 8

Just Because

You don't need a reason to send a handmade greeting! Here are lots of ideas for cards you can send 'just because,' to let loved ones know you care.

Birthday

What occasion is celebrated more than any other? Birthdays! Check out these fun ideas for birthday greetings you can make yourself.

A Day of Adventure,
page 54

Monogrammed Note Cards,
page 18

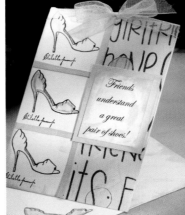

A Great Pair of Shoes,
page 32

Friendship in Bloom,
page 42

Birthday Balloons,
page 58

CONTENTS

**Stitched Thanks,
page 90**

**Celebrate, Wish, Dream,
page 62**

**Christmas Peace,
page 142**

Envelope Templates

Between the Covers

Four Seasons, page 113

Patchwork Quilting

Quilting is a centuries-old tradition that has been resurrected in modern-age popularity. We present you with some of the most colourful and lovely patterns any quilter would be proud to create. There was a great revival of quilting in the 1920s and its popularity continued through the depression. It is again one of the most popular crafts. Patchwork Quilting will help you create a stitch in time!

{Hello}, page 10

Card Making
Handmade Greetings for All Occasions

With every card you make, you truly give a bit of yourself in the process. Making your own cards is a fun, creative and less costly way of letting someone know how you really feel. Have you ever looked at a handmade card and thought to yourself, "this is really lovely! I wish I knew how to make my own greeting cards." Well now you can! Making greeting cards is truly fun with Card Making as your guide. Buy it now and we'll show you how!

Counterpane Log Afghan, page 120

Knitting
Easy Fun for Everyone

Knitting has enjoyed a surge in popularity over the last few years as more people take up a craft that was once thought of as grandma's hobby. Knitting allows you to make all sorts of useful and beautiful things with a couple needles and some yarn. It's also a great way to occupy your hands while talking, watching a movie or doing almost anything. For beautiful projects, our knitting book is a must have to expand your purls of wisdom!

For more information about Company's Coming craft books, visit our website, www.companyscoming.com

FOREWORD

It's quick, easy and fun. It doesn't take a ton of specialized equipment or supplies. And it can be done well by just about anyone! It's card making—the trend that's taking the crafting world by storm.

With only a bit of card stock, a sticker or a rubber stamp, and a few simple embellishments, you can show that special someone just how much you care with a lovely handmade greeting card.

With these step-by-step instructions, full-colour photography and your own creativity, it won't take long until you are making beautiful card creations for any occasion. These all-occasion cards are designed in a variety of styles from light-hearted and whimsical to elegant and sophisticated.

You don't need a reason to send a handmade card. Sometimes you want to send one for no reason at all, just to tell someone 'I'm thinking of you' or to encourage them in a difficult time or simply to tell them how happy you are to be friends.

Birthdays are celebrated more often than any other event, so we have included an extra-special selection of birthday cards for all ages.

Life's special events deserve special cards too, and in this book you'll find cards for new babies, weddings, graduations and more, as well as a variety of thank-you cards. There are even cards for those occasions when you have to say 'I'm sorry.'

You'll also find an astounding array of holiday cards from St. Patrick's Day to Christmas, and almost everything in between. As a bonus, we've included templates for four of the most popular envelope sizes, so you can create a co-ordinated finishing touch to every handmade greeting.

Wishing you creative card making!

A Purse Full of Cards, page 22

Floral Sympathy, page 84

Cutting and Tearing

Craft knife, cutting mat Must-have tools. Mat protects work surface, keeps blades from getting dull.

Measure and mark Diagrams show solid lines for cutting, dotted lines for folding.

Other cutters Guillotine and rotary-blade paper cutters, oval and circle cutters, cutters that cut unusual shapes via a gear or cam system, swivel-blade knives that cut along the channels of plastic templates, and die cutting machines (large or small in size and price). Markers that draw as they cut.

Punches Available in hundreds of shapes and sizes ranging from 1/16 inch to over 3 inches (use for eyelets, lettering, dimensional punch art, and embellishments). Also punches for two-ring, three-ring, coil, comb and disk binding.

Scissors Long and short blades that cut straight or a pattern. Scissors with non-stick coating are ideal for cutting adhesive sheets and tape, bonsai scissors best for cutting rubber or heavy board. Consider comfort—large holes for fingers, soft grips.

Tearing Tear paper for collage, special effects, layering on cards, scrapbook pages and more. Wet a small paintbrush; tear along the wet line for a deckle edge.

Embellishments

If you are not already a pack rat, it is time to start! Embellish projects with stickers, eyelets, brads, nail heads, wire, beads, iron-on ribbon and braid, memorabilia and printed ephemera.

Embossing

Dry embossing Use a light source, stencil, card stock and stylus tool. Add colour, or leave raised areas plain.

Heat embossing Use embossing powder, ink, card stock and a heat tool to create raised designs and textures. Powders come in a wide range of colours. Fine grain is called 'detail' and heavier called 'ultrathick.' Embossing powders will not stick to most dye inks—use pigment inks or special clear embossing inks for best results.

Glues and Adhesives

Basics Each glue or adhesive is formulated for a particular use and specified surfaces. Read the label and carefully follow directions, especially those that involve personal safety and health.

Foam tape Adds dimension.

Glue dots, adhesive sheets and cartridge type machines Quick grab, no drying time needed.

Glue pens Fine line control.

Glue sticks Wide coverage.

Repositionable products Useful for stencils and temporary holding.

Measuring

Rulers A metal straightedge for cutting with a craft knife (a must-have tool). Match the length of the ruler to the project (shorter rulers are easier to use when working on smaller projects).
Quilter's grid ruler Use to measure squares and rectangles.

Paper and Card Stock

Card stock Heavier and stiffer than paper. A sturdy surface for cards, boxes, ornaments.
Paper Lighter weight surfaces used for drawing, stamping, collage.
Storage and organization Store paper flat and away from moisture. Arrange by colour, size or type. Keep your scraps for collage projects.
Types Handmade, milled, marbled, mulberry, origami, embossed, glossy, matte, botanical inclusions, vellum, parchment, preprinted, tissue and more.

Pens and Markers

Inks (permanent, watercolour, metallic, etc.), **colours** (sold by sets or individually), **and nibs** (fine point, calligraphy, etc.) **to suit the project.** For journals and scrapbooks, make sure inks are permanent and fade-resistant.
Store pens and markers flat unless the manufacturer says otherwise.

Scoring and Folding

Folding Mountain folds—up, valley folds—down. Most patterns will have different types of dotted lines to denote mountain or valley folds.

Tools Scoring tool and bone folder. Fingernails will scar the surface of the paper.

Stamping

Direct-to-paper (DTP) Use ink pad, sponge or stylus tool to apply ink instead of a rubber stamp.
Inks Available in pads and re-inker bottles. Types include dye and pigment, permanent, waterproof and fade resistant or archival, chalk finish, fast drying, slow drying, rainbow and more. Read the labels to determine what is best for a project or surface.
Make stamps Carve rubber, erasers, carving blocks or vegetables. Heat Magic Stamp foam blocks to press against textures. Stamp found objects such as leaves and flowers, keys and coins, etc.
Stamps Sold mounted on wood, acrylic or foam, or unmounted (rubber part only), made from vulcanized rubber, acrylic or foam.
Store Flat and away from light and heat.
Techniques Tap the ink onto the stamp (using the pad as the applicator) or tap the stamp onto the ink pad. Stamp with even hand pressure (no rocking) for best results. For very large stamps, apply ink with a brayer. Colour the surface of a stamp with watercolour markers (several colours), huff with breath to keep the colours moist, then stamp; or lightly spray with water mist before stamping for a very different effect.
Unmounted stamps Mount temporarily on acrylic blocks with Scotch Poster Tape on one surface (nothing on the rubber stamp) or one of the other methods (hook and loop tape, paint on adhesives, cling plastic).

{Hello}

Raid your button jar for dimensional accents to a single-panel card.

DESIGN BY XENIA FEERE

Materials

Card stock: kraft, light sage green
Various printed papers
Light blue envelope to fit a 5½-inch-square card
Black rub-on transfers: quotation marks, brackets
Black fine-tip marker
Black dye ink pad
11 round buttons
1-inch circle punch
Tacky glue
Paper adhesive
Computer and printer (optional)

Project note: This is a single-panel card, but it can easily be made into a two-panel card by cutting a 5½ x 11-inch piece of kraft card stock and folding it in half.

Cut a 5½-inch square from kraft card stock. Hand-print, or use a computer to generate, 'Hello' on light sage green card stock; cut a 3⅛-inch square around word. Apply bracket rub-on transfers to each side of word. Ink edges of square. Adhere to upper left corner of kraft square.

Punch twenty-one 1-inch circles from various printed papers; ink edges of each circle. Referring to photo, adhere 16 circles to kraft square. Use tacky glue to adhere a button to every other circle.

Apply quotation mark rub-on transfers to upper left and lower right corners of reverse side of square.

Adhere the five remaining circles to bottom edge of envelope front; adhere a button to every other circle. ■

SOURCES: Printed papers from 7gypsies, Scenic Route Paper Co., Autumn Leaves, Scrapworks, KI Memories, Li'l Davis Designs, K&Company, Lasting Impressions for Paper Inc. and Paper Adventures/ANW Crestwood; rub-on transfers from Autumn Leaves.

reverse side

Floral Mosaic Card

Patterned paper becomes a dramatic focal point when cut into strips of random widths.

DESIGN BY CATHY SHELLENBERG

Materials
Card stock: pink, brown
Pink/brown floral-printed paper
Metal-rimmed tag
'thinking of you' rubber stamp
Ink pads: brown, black
½-inch-wide pink ribbon
Small hole punch
Paper glue

Cut pink card stock to 5½ x 8½ inches; fold in half to make 5½ x 4¼-inch top-fold card.

Cut brown card stock to 5¼ x 4 inches. Cut floral printed paper to 4 x 3¼ inches. To create mosaic effect, cut floral rectangle into 11 random strips with alternate diagonal directions. **Note:** *Keep strips in order they are cut.*

Ink edges of floral strips with brown. Reassemble and adhere strips to brown card stock, leaving a slight space between each piece.

Cut a piece of brown card stock to fit inside rim of tag. With black ink, stamp 'thinking of you' on tag. Punch a small hole in top of tag.

Cut two lengths of ribbon; knot two ends together. Insert remaining ends from front to back through hole in tag, pulling tag close to knot, and then wrap around brown card stock and adhere.

Adhere brown card stock to front of card. ∎

Pretty in Plaid

A small silk flower softens the strong diagonal lines of this easy-to-make card.

DESIGN BY CATHY SHELLENBERG

Materials
Card stock: pink, brown
Pink/brown plaid printed paper
'thinking of you' rubber stamp
Brown ink pad
1½-inch round pink die-cut tag
½-inch-wide pink ribbon
Coil clips
Brads: large pink, small pewter
Brown paper blossom
⅜-inch-wide ribbon
Small hole punch
Paper glue

Cut pink card stock 5½ x 8½ inches; fold in half to make 5½ x 4¼-inch card.

Cut brown card stock 5¼ x 4 inches. Cut printed paper 5 x 3¾ inches.

Loop a length of ribbon through one coil clip; adhere ribbon ends on back of brown card stock, leaving a length of ribbon on front of card. Repeat on opposite side of card. Slip ends of another length of ribbon through clips and knot together taught across front of card.

Ink edges of die-cut tag; stamp 'thinking of you.' Adhere tag to lower right corner of printed card stock by inserting large pink brad through coil clip and tag. Attach brown blossom to lower edge of tag with small pewter brad.

Adhere brown card stock to front of card. ■

Fruits of Summer

Ease into quilling with these simple fruit shapes.

DESIGNS BY SUSAN STRINGFELLOW

Materials

Card stock: green, yellow, white, dark pink, black,
   light orange
Printed papers: multicoloured striped,
   strawberries, pears, cherries, oranges
4 vellum envelopes to fit 4¼ x 5½-inch cards
4 chipboard circle coasters
Rubber stamps: alphabet, small dot
Black pearlescent ink pad
Black fine-tip marker
⅜-inch-wide black with white stitches ribbon
4 brads in assorted colours
Sandpaper
Slotted quilling tool
Punches: 1½-inch circle, ¹⁄₁₆-inch hole
Glue stick
Clear-drying adhesive

*Project note: Refer to quilling patterns when
quilling shapes. Secure ends of quilled pieces with
clear-drying adhesive; let dry.*

   Cut an 8½ x 5½-inch rectangle of yellow or
green card stock; score and fold in half, forming
a 4¼ x 5½-inch card. Using alphabet stamps and
black ink, stamp name of fruit along left edge
of card front a few times, stamping a small dot
between each word.
   Adhere a 3½ x 5¼-inch piece of multicoloured
striped paper to right side of card. Using a coaster
as a template, cut a circle from fruit printed paper;
adhere paper to coaster and sand edges. Referring
to photo for placement, adhere coaster to left side
of card front.
   Punch a 1½-inch circle from white card stock;

draw a thin black line along circle edge. Adhere to
coaster on card. Fold a 2¼-inch length of ribbon
in half; place folded end of ribbon on white circle
and punch a ¹⁄₁₆-inch hole through all layers;
insert a brad, securing ribbon to card. Following
instructions below and referring to patterns,
assemble desired quilled fruit and adhere to white
circle on card front.
   For **quilled strawberry**, cut a ⅛ x 12-inch strip of
dark pink card stock. Use slotted quilling tool to form
a strawberry. Use provided pattern to trace and cut
strawberry leaf from green card stock; adhere to top
of strawberry.
   For **quilled cherry**, cut a ⅛ x 8-inch strip of dark
pink card stock. Use slotted quilling tool to form a
cherry. Cut a ⅛ x 4-inch strip of green card stock;
use slotted quilling tool to form a leaf, pinching
ends for desired shape. Cut a ¹⁄₁₆ x ¾-inch strip from
black card stock; adhere ends of strip to quilled
cherry and leaf for a stem.
   For **quilled orange**, cut three ⅛ x 6-inch strips
from light orange card stock. Use slotted quilling
tool to form strips into three orange sections.
Adhere orange sections together, forming an
orange wedge. Form a leaf from a ⅛ x 4-inch strip
of green card stock, pinching ends for desired
shape; adhere leaf to orange wedge.
   For **quilled pear**, cut a ⅛ x 12-inch strip of
yellow card stock. Use slotted quilling tool to
form a pear. Form a leaf from a ⅛ x 4-inch strip of
green card stock, pinching ends for desired shape;
adhere to pear. Cut a ¹⁄₁₆ x ⅜-inch strip from black
card stock; adhere to top of pear for a stem.
   For envelopes, cut four 6 x 1-inch strips from
multicoloured striped paper; centre and adhere

to top envelope flaps. Trim edges even. Punch
a 1½-inch circle from each of the fruit printed
papers; sand edges and adhere circles to centres
of multicoloured striped papers on envelope
flaps. ■

SOURCES: Printed papers from SEI; coasters from Altered Pages; vellum envelopes from
Die Cuts With A View; rubber stamps from Hero Arts; ink pad from Jacquard Products;
clear-drying adhesive from JudiKins.

Fruits of Summer
Leaf

Fruits of Summer
Pear

Fruits of Summer
Orange Section

Fruits of Summer
Cherry

Fruits of Summer
Strawberry

Fruits of Summer
Strawberry Leaf

Monogrammed Note Cards

Easy paper weaving creates an elegant look on this sophisticated set.

DESIGNS BY KAREN DESMET

Materials

Card stock: white, light pink
Printed papers: pink, light green, green, cream/
    purple, purple, cream floral, yellow, green floral,
    pink floral
Co-ordinating floral die cuts
White envelopes to fit 4¼ x 5½-inch cards
Initial rub-on transfers
Initial foam stamp
Light green dye ink pad
Satin bows with ribbon tails: pale pink, cream
1-inch-wide satin ribbon: cream, green, pale pink
Metal-edge vellum square tag
Adhesive foam tape
Adhesive applicator with permanent adhesive
cartridges

Project note: For each card, first cut a 5½ x 8½-inch piece of white card stock; score and fold in half. The woven cards have a side fold; remaining cards have a top fold.

Woven Cards: For pink/light green card, cut nine ⅝-inch-wide strips from light green printed paper; cut seven ⅝-inch-wide strips from pink printed paper. Place one light green strip horizontal on work surface and one pink strip vertical on work surface; line up the top corner of pink strip with the left corner of light green strip and adhere. Continue adhering pink strips vertically to light green strip,

lining up top edges and alternating between adhering pink strips on top of light green strip and on back of light green strip, forming an over-and-under pattern. Weave the light green strips through the pink strips. Adhere woven panel to card front; trim edges even.

Cut a 5¾-inch length of pink ribbon; cut one end on diagonal then adhere straight end to top centre of card front. Adhere pink satin bow over top of ribbon. Transfer initial rub-on to white card stock. Cut a rectangle around initial and layer it onto light pink card stock. Trim a narrow border. Adhere to card.

For cream/green card, follow instructions above, but use green and cream/purple printed papers. Use cream ribbon and cream satin bow instead of pink and transfer initial to ribbon length.

Floral Cards: Adhere yellow or green printed paper to card front; trim edges even. For yellow card, adhere a 2⅝-inch-wide strip of green floral printed paper to bottom portion of card front; trim edges even. Use foam tape to adhere co-ordinating floral die cut to card. Stamp initial on lower right corner of card; trace initial with a pencil.

For pink card, adhere a 2¾ x 4¼-inch piece of pink floral printed paper to left side of card front, cutting paper so a floral image is near the right edge of strip. Adhere pale pink satin ribbon to left edge of card; trim edges even. Use foam tape to adhere co-ordinating floral die cut to card, slightly overlapping

floral image on printed paper. Transfer initial rub-on to lower right corner of card.

For envelopes, use top envelope flaps as templates to trace and cut pieces of co-ordinating printed papers to fit. Adhere papers to top envelope flaps. ■

SOURCES: Printed papers, die cuts and satin bows from Anna Griffin Inc.; rub-on transfers from me & my BIG ideas and Doodlebug Design Inc.; adhesive applicator and cartridges from Xyron.

Little Notes

A little white paint and a small square embellishment add up to big impact in this card set.

DESIGNS BY GRETCHEN SCHMIDT

Materials
3-inch square olive green cards with envelopes
Brightly coloured acrylic square embellishments
Alphabet rubber stamps
Black pigment ink pad
Clear embossing powder
Acrylic paints: white, orange, red, blue, lime green
⅛-inch-wide red polka-dot ribbon
Orange rickrack
Highlighter marker cap
Embossing heat tool
⅛-inch hole punch
Foam brush
Adhesive dots

Using a foam brush, lightly apply white paint to centre section of each card in a swiping motion. Let dry. Stamp desired sentiments at bottom of each card; sprinkle letters with clear embossing powder and emboss. Use adhesive dots to attach a square embellishment to each.

To decorate envelopes, use a highlighter marker cap and acrylic paints to stamp desired number of circles in assorted colours on envelope fronts. Let dry. If desired, punch a ⅛-inch hole through corner of envelope and thread rickrack or ribbon through hole. Tie a knot and trim ends. ■

SOURCES: Cards from Die Cuts With A View; acrylic embellishments from KI Memories; rubber stamps from K&Company.

A Purse Full of Cards

An embellished wooden purse filled with matching note cards makes a perfect gift!

DESIGNS BY LINDA BEESON

Materials

Wooden purse
Card stock: brown, pink, white
Lounge collection printed papers
Co-ordinating circle tag
Rubber stamps: initial, monogram circle
Brown dye ink pad
Chipboard flower
Copper charms
Ribbon: 1-inch-wide brown with pink polka dots,
   ⅞-inch-wide pink striped
Brown acrylic paint
Sandpaper
Circle punches: scallop-edge, 1½-inch, 1¾-inch
Foam brush
Crystal lacquer
Adhesive foam tape
Découpage medium

Paint the purse brown, inside and out; let inside dry completely before closing. Repeat for a second coat, if needed.

Cut pieces of printed papers to fit front and back of purse; use foam brush and découpage medium to adhere papers to purse. Cut two 1¾-inch-wide strips of a different printed paper; adhere to front and back of purse in the same manner as before. Trim edges even.

Punch a scallop-edge circle from brown card stock; adhere circle tag to scallop-edge circle and adhere to front of purse. Brush découpage medium over entire purse, making sure purse is kept open until completely dry.

Adhere printed paper to chipboard flower; trim edges even. Sand edges; brush on a thin layer of crystal lacquer. Let dry. Attach copper charms to flower centre; adhere to purse on top of circle tag. Tie ribbon onto handle as desired; trim ribbon ends.

Form four 4½ x 4⅜-inch top-folded cards from brown card stock. Cut four rectangles from printed papers slightly smaller than card fronts; adhere a rectangle to each card.

Stamp initial four times on white card stock; stamp monogram circle around each initial. Punch a 1½-inch circle around each monogram. Punch four 1¾-inch circles from pink card stock and four scallop-edge circles from brown card stock. Layer and adhere monogram circles on top of pink circles; adhere pink circles on top of scallop-edge circles. Adhere circles to cards with foam tape, placing a folded ribbon loop underneath each circle.

For envelopes, cut four 6¾-inch squares from brown card stock. Position each square as a diamond and fold the corners in toward the centre until they meet, forming envelopes. ■

SOURCES: Printed papers, circle tag, rubber stamps and ink pad from Paper Salon Inc.; wooden purse from DecoArt; chipboard flower from Maya Road; copper charms from Nunn Design; scallop-edge circle punch from Uchida of America; decoupage medium from Plaid Enterprises; crystal lacquer from Sakura of America.

Flower Stationery Set

Easy stamped images make a simple, yet stunning set.

DESIGNS BY KIM HUGHES

Materials
White card stock
Create-a-Flower Tailored Tin stamp set
Ink pads: key lime, pear, lipstick, flamingo, coffee
   bean, creamsicle, periwinkle
Yellow ribbon
Flower soft charm

Cut four 8 x 4½-inch pieces from white card stock and fold to create four side-fold cards.

Using key lime ink pad, stamp sentiment from Tailored Tin on bottom front of each card.

Using coffee bean ink pad, stamp one stem vertically on each card centred just above sentiment.

Using ink pads as desired, mix and match stamps to create four different flower shapes.

Stack cards and tie ribbon around with the flower charm tie on to front knot. ■

SOURCES: Create-a-Flower Tailored Tin and ink pads from Paper Salon Inc.; Soft Charm from Around The Block.

Just for You Cards

This note card set can be made assembly-line style, changing only the colours and placement of embellishments.

DESIGNS BY SHARON REINHART

Materials
White card stock
Double-sided printed card stock: striped/lavender, cubed/pink
White envelopes to fit 3-inch-square cards
3½-inch-square acetate box
Sentiment rubber stamps
Black dye ink pad
⅛-inch-wide satin ribbon, desired colours
Punches: tag, southwest corner, ¹⁄₁₆-inch hole
Removable adhesive
Adhesive foam tape
Paper adhesive

Form desired number of 3-inch-square top-folded cards from striped/lavender card stock. Punch a tag from white card stock for each card; adhere a ⅜-inch-wide strip of striped/lavender card stock to the bottom of each tag. Trim edges even. Stamp a sentiment on each tag above printed card stock.

Cut a 2-inch square from cubed/pink card stock for each card; punch corners of squares with southwest corner punch. Adhere tags to squares, positioning some squares as diamonds. Punch two ¹⁄₁₆-inch holes next to each other through bottom area of each tag; tie ribbon through each set of holes. Trim ribbon ends. Use foam tape to adhere

assembled panels to cards.

To decorate envelopes, cut 2-inch squares from cubed/pink card stock; punch corners with southwest punch and adhere one square to each envelope.

For box, cut a 5½-inch square from striped/lavender card stock; score a line 1 inch from each edge. Referring to Fig. 1, cut out corners. Adhere a note card to centre of square with removable adhesive so card can be used later; fold on scored lines and insert inside box lid. Cut a piece of striped/lavender card stock to fit bottom of box; place inside box base. Place envelopes and cards inside box. ∎

SOURCES: Printed card stock from American Crafts; rubber stamps from Hero Arts; acetate box from Creative Packaging Inc.

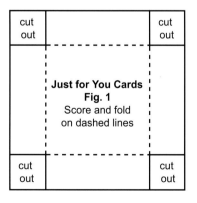

cut out		cut out
	Just for You Cards **Fig. 1** Score and fold on dashed lines	
cut out		cut out

Just for You

You're a Great Friend!

With Loving Thoughts

Hello from the Heart

Flower Card Set

Showcase your favourite flower photos with this springtime-fresh set.

DESIGNS BY KATHLEEN PANEITZ

Materials

Card stock: green, light blue, pink, white, black

White envelopes to fit 5½ x 4¼-inch cards (optional)

3 x 4-inch flower photos

Floral transparency

Clear words and flower stickers

Rub-on transfers: flowers, black alphabet, white alphabet

29 inches ½-inch-wide pink with white handwriting printed ribbon

Stapler with yellow staples

Die-cutting machine with Portfolio (#P1494) die

Craft knife

Paper adhesive

Die-cut a portfolio from green card stock; assemble portfolio. With craft knife, cut ⅝-inch-long slits along folds on front and back of portfolio just below centre. Thread ribbon through slits.

Cut a piece of light blue card stock to fit front of portfolio; adhere to holder. Decorate front of portfolio with stickers, rub-on transfers and a flower photo.

Trim floral transparency to fit one bottom flap inside portfolio; staple transparency to bottom flap. Decorate inside with stickers and rub-on transfers; use rub-on transfers to spell desired words inside portfolio.

For postcards, adhere flower photos to white or black card stock; trim a small border around each. Adhere photos to 5½ x 4¼-inch pieces of pink and light blue card stock. Add greetings below photos with rub-on transfers. Place postcards and envelopes (if desired) inside portfolio. ■

SOURCES: Die-cutting machine and die from AccuCut; stickers and transparency from Autumn Leaves; flower rub-on transfers from QuicKutz Inc.; alphabet rub-on transfers and staples from Making Memories; ribbon from Creative Imaginations; paper adhesive from Beacon Adhesives Inc.

Get Well Soon

Send get-well wishes with an unusual wedge-shaped card.

DESIGN BY TAMI MAYBERRY

Materials
Card stock: pink, dark pink
Pink striped printed paper
2 light orange fabric flowers
'Get Well Soon' metal circle embellishment
Get-well-themed sentiment sticker
3½ inches ½-inch-wide orange grosgrain ribbon
FreeStyle Wedge card and envelope templates kit
Paper adhesive

Use card template to cut a side-folded card from dark pink card stock. Use the same template to cut just a card front from pink striped paper; cut off right 1¼ inches in a wavy pattern; adhere to card front as shown. Adhere ribbon to card 2¼ inches from top.

Layer flowers and adhere to card as shown; adhere 'Get Well Soon' metal embellishment to flower centre.

Use card template to cut a side-folded card from pink card stock; with card closed, cut ⅛ inch off right edge and adhere inside dark pink card, aligning folds. Attach sentiment sticker inside card.

Use envelope template to cut an envelope from pink striped paper; assemble envelope. ∎

SOURCES: Templates kit from Green Sneakers Inc.; printed paper and flowers from Doodlebug Design Inc.; metal embellishment from Magic Scraps; sticker from K&Company.

SENDING YOU
LOTS OF
LOVE
& get well wishes

A Great Pair of Shoes

Fabulous footwear is essential to life, and your best girlfriends understand that!

DESIGN BY KAREN DESMET

Materials

Card stock: cream, light sage green
Julie's Thoughts printed paper
Cream envelope to fit a 4¼ x 5½-inch card
Black fine-tip marker
Stiletto rubber stamp
Ink pads: black solvent-based, tan distress
Green watercolour crayon
½-inch-wide gold sheer ribbon
Waterbrush or craft sponge
Adhesive foam tape
Paper adhesive
Computer and printer (optional)

Form a 4¼ x 5½-inch top-folded card from cream card stock. Adhere a 2⅛ x 5½-inch piece of Julie's Thoughts printed paper to right side of card. Cut three strips of light sage green card stock, one measuring ³⁄₁₆ x 5½ inches and two measuring 2⅛ x ³⁄₁₆ inches. Adhere long strip to left edge of printed paper on card; adhere short strips horizontally to left side of card, aligning left edges and forming three boxes.

Stamp stiletto image inside each box with black ink; colour centre stiletto with watercolour crayon, using a slightly damp sponge or blender pen to blend colour. Let dry. Ink card edges with tan distress ink.

Hand-print, or use a computer to generate, 'Friends understand a great pair of shoes!' on cream card stock; cut a 1⅞ x 2-inch rectangle around words. Ink edges with tan distress ink and adhere to light sage green card stock; trim a small border and adhere to right side of card front with foam tape. Wrap ribbon through fold of card and tie a bow on front; trim ribbon ends.

Decorate envelope by stamping stiletto on lower left corner with black ink and colouring in the same manner as for card; let dry. Ink edges with tan distress ink. ■

SOURCES: Printed paper from Rusty Pickle; rubber stamp from American Art Stamp; solvent-based ink pad from Tsukineko Inc.; distress ink pad from Ranger Industries Inc.

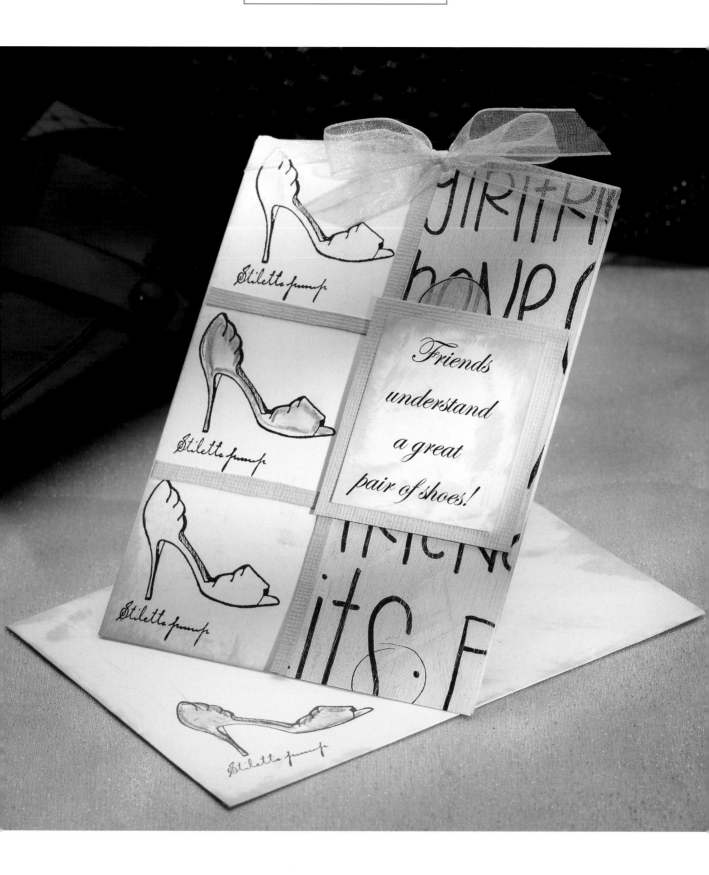

Tulip Pot

Layered papers in springtime colours frame a single stamped image.

DESIGN BY STEPHANIE BARNARD

Materials
White card stock
Printed papers: light green stitched, pink swirl,
   blue polka-dot
Rubber stamps: vase, tulip and greenery
Black dye ink pad
Watercolours
Paintbrush
Die-cutting tool and envelope die or envelope
   template from page 154
Double-sided tape *or* glue stick

   Cut a 6¾ x 9⅝-inch piece of white card stock; score and fold in half, forming a 6¾ x 4¾-inch card. Centre and adhere the following printed papers to card front in the following order: a 6½ x 4½-inch piece of light green stitched printed paper, a 6½ x 3¼-inch piece of pink swirl printed paper and a 4½ x 4½-inch piece of blue polka-dot printed paper.

   Stamp vase on white card stock; use stamped vase as a template to trace and cut a vase shape from white card stock. Place white vase on top of stamped vase to act as a mask and then stamp the tulip and greenery, positioning them so they look like they have been placed inside vase. Watercolour image and let dry. Cut a 2½ x 3¾-inch rectangle around image; centre and adhere to card.

   Form envelope from white card stock using die-cutter and die, or enlarge and trace template from page 154. Cut three rectangles from printed papers in various sizes to fit left side of envelope; adhere rectangles to envelope front. ■

SOURCES: Printed papers from American Traditional Designs; rubber stamps from Plaid Enterprises/All Night Media; die-cutting tool and envelope die from Ellison.

Happy Place

Send a friend to her 'happy place' when she needs a bit of encouragement.

DESIGN BY ASELA HOPKINS

Materials

Card stock: sage green, white, black, lavender
Rubber stamps: All Natural set (includes large flower), Cute Converse set (includes 'happy place'), Taking A Stroll (girl with umbrella)
Dye ink pads: lavender, yellow, purple, pink, green, light green, orange, black
Black solvent-based ink pad
Watermark ink pad
Embossing powders: lavender, pink
Coloured pencils
Black fine-tip permanent marker
Clear ultra-fine glitter
Small watercolour brush
Embossing heat tool
Adhesive foam squares
Glue stick
Clear-drying liquid glue

Form a 4¼ x 5½-inch side-folded card from sage green card stock. Use watermark ink to stamp large flowers randomly on card; emboss each with pink or lavender embossing powder.

Use black solvent-based ink to stamp girl with umbrella onto a 2⅜ x 4¾-inch piece of white card stock. Stamp just the top part of the umbrella onto a scrap piece of white card stock. Use dye inks and coloured pencils to colour both images, beginning with lighter colours first. Use watercolour brush when using dye inks. Let dry.

Cut out the top part of umbrella and set aside. Randomly draw raindrops, flowers and grass beside girl with black fine-tip marker. Colour flowers in the same manner as previous images. Apply small amounts of clear-drying glue to raindrops and sprinkle on glitter; let dry. Stamp 'happy place' on lower right corner with black dye ink.

Ink edges with lavender ink. Adhere to lavender card stock and trim a narrow border; adhere to black card stock; trim a narrow border. Use foam dots to adhere single umbrella to top part on umbrella that girl is holding. Adhere assembled panel to card. ■

SOURCES: Rubber stamp sets, dye ink pads and embossing powders from Stampin' Up!; Taking A Stroll rubber stamp from Inky Antics; solvent-based and watermark ink pads from Tsukineko Inc.

Rustic Florals

Gentle distressing with sandpaper and ink create a well-worn look in this all-occasion set.

DESIGN BY WENDY MALICHIO

Materials
White card stock
Barn Wood printed papers: green, ochre, red
Black printed paper
Stickers: flowers, twill sentiment stickers
Flower die cuts
Fine-tip markers (optional)
Brown distress ink pad
3 floral brads
¼-inch-wide golden yellow ombré ribbon
Sandpaper
Pocket template
Punches: 1-inch circle, ¼-inch hole, ¹⁄₁₆-inch hole
Corner rounder
Computer with Microsoft Word

Use a computer to generate desired sentiment over and over, filling a 4 x 5¼-inch area; use Word Art feature in software program to generate one large sentiment on top of small sentiments. Print text on white card stock. **Option:** *Hand-print sentiments on white card stock.*

For pocket insert, cut a 4 x 5¼-inch rectangle from printed card stock; round corners. Cut a 4 x 1¾-inch-wide strip of black printed paper; tear off top edge and ink edges. Adhere to insert. Ink edges. Attach a flower sticker. Punch a ¼-inch hole through centre top of insert; tie on ribbon. Trim ribbon ends. Set aside.

Use template to cut a pocket from Barn Wood printed paper; assemble envelope. Sand and ink edges. Punch a half circle at centre top on front of pocket with 1-inch circle punch.

Cut desired-size piece of black printed paper; tear off top and bottom edges diagonally. Ink edges as desired and adhere to pocket. Crumple flower die cut; smooth out and sand lightly. Adhere to pocket. Trim edges of twill sentiment sticker as desired; ink edges. Punch a ¹⁄₁₆-inch hole through centre top and insert a brad. Attach sticker to pocket. Place insert inside pocket.

Repeat to make two more pockets and inserts. ■

SOURCES: Printed papers, twill stickers, die cuts and ribbon from Paper House Productions; distress ink pad from Ranger Industries Inc.; pocket template from Provo Craft/Coluzzle.

Congratulations

Hello Friend!

Relax
Reflect
Renew

A
flower
touches
everyone's
heart.

O'KEEFE

Happy Mother's Day

Between Friends

Send your love across the miles with a simply elegant stamped card.

DESIGN BY JULIE EBERSOLE

Materials

Card stock: white, pale yellow, pale peach
Envelope to fit 4¼-inch-square card
Rubber stamps: house with trees, small house, decorative swirl, ¾-inch-diameter solid circle, friend sentiment
Ink pads: black pigment, yellow dye
Markers
2 black mini round brads
Ribbon: ⅛-inch-wide black with white stitching
Punches: half circle slit, rounded corner
Glue stick

Cut a 4¼ x 8½-inch piece of pale yellow card stock; score and fold in half, forming a 4¼-inch square card. Punch a half-circle slit ¾ inch in from each side on card front, with curves of half circles facing each other.

Using black ink, stamp house with trees on white card stock; use yellow ink to stamp solid circle to the upper right area above house. Colour house and trees with markers. Cut a 2½ x 2¼-inch rectangle around images, cutting off top edge of stamped circle; glue to pale peach card stock. Trim a small border.

Wrap ribbon around upper left and lower right corners of layered image. Knot ends in upper left corner to secure; trim ends. Slide layered image into punched slits on card front.

Punch a 1/16-inch hole through centre of each half circle slit and through stamped panel; insert brads. ■

SOURCES: Rubber stamps from A Muse Artstamps; printed paper from Chatterbox Inc.; slit punch from Stampin' Up!

THE ROAD TO A FRIEND'S HOUSE IS NEVER *long* - Danish Proverb

Friendship in Bloom

Acrylic craft paint provides a textural background for the stamped tag.

DESIGN BY LISA JOHNSON

Materials

Card stock: turquoise, matte white, shimmery
  white, pink, pale orange
Envelope to fit a 4⅛ x 5⅜-inch card
Word cutouts: 2 friendship-themed sentiments
Flowers rubber stamp
Black dye ink pad
Acrylic paint: bright green, pink, blue, orange
¼-inch-wide pink grosgrain ribbon
Silver cord
3 silver seed beads
2 spiral clips
2 orange eyelets with eyelet-setting tool
Hole punches: ½-, ¼- and ⅛-inch
Rounded slit punch
Paintbrush
Foam brush
Glue stick
Adhesive foam dots
Clear-drying adhesive

Cut an 8¼ x 5⅜-inch piece of turquoise card stock; score and fold in half to form a 4⅛ x 5⅜-inch card. Use foam brush to paint a sheet of matte white card stock and envelope bright green, applying the paint in a swiping motion; let dry.

Cut a 2 x 2⅝-inch piece of turquoise card stock; trim top corners diagonally, forming a tag. Punch centre top with slit punch. Punch a ½-inch circle from painted card stock; adhere to centre top of tag. Punch a ⅛-inch hole through centre of circle; set eyelet. Insert ribbon through eyelet and tie a knot; trim ribbon ends.

Cut a 1¾ x 2-inch rectangle from shimmery white card stock; stamp flower image onto rectangle. Paint flowers; let dry. Use clear-drying adhesive to adhere seed beads to flower centres. Let dry. Slide underneath slit on tag and adhere. Adhere a word cutout to tag and slide on spiral clip.

Cut a 4 x 5¼-inch piece of painted card stock; centre and adhere to card front. Use foam dots to adhere assembled tag to card front. Punch ¼-inch circles from pink, blue and pale orange card stocks; adhere to lower right corner of card.

To embellish envelope, adhere word cutout to turquoise card stock; cut a rectangle around words, allowing additional space on ends. Punch a ½-inch circle from painted card stock and adhere to right end; punch a ⅛-inch hole through circle and set eyelet. Thread ribbon through eyelet and tie a knot; trim ends and tie silver cord onto ribbon. Slide spiral clip onto left end of card stock. Adhere assembled piece to left end of envelope. ■

SOURCES: Rubber stamps, word cutouts, clips, card stock, ink pad and clear adhesive from Stampin' Up!

To My Friend

An accordion-fold card for a special friend features mini manila index cards.

DESIGN BY LORI BROFSKY

Materials

Ivory card stock
2 (8 x 5-inch) manila index card dividers
Variety of pink printed papers
White paper
Flash cards: 'always,' 'laugh,' 'friend'
Rub-on transfers: black alphabet, pink 'A'
'F' monogram
Chipboard ampersand
Tape measure rubber stamp
Dye ink pads: pink, brown, black
Vintage plastic sewing tool
Pink ribbons
Black fine-tip marker (optional)
Rickrack stickers
Paper flowers: 1 large, 4 small
Black button
Brads: 4 gold mini, 1 large pewter
Sandpaper
Circle punches: 1-, 1⅛- and 1½-inch
Craft sponges
Craft knife
Stapler with staples
Adhesive foam tape
Adhesive dots
Paper adhesive
Computer and printer

Project note: *Sand edges of all pieces as desired.*

Fold index card dividers in half and adhere together, forming a three-panel accordion-folded card. Adhere printed papers to front and back of each panel; trim edges even.

Punch three 1-inch circles from printed papers; punch 1½-inch circles around punched circles off-centre, forming circle frames. Adhere to card front. Attach a rickrack sticker to bottom.

Apply alphabet rub-on transfers to 'F' monogram to spell 'Friend.' Tie two ribbons onto letter; trim ribbon ends. Use foam tape to adhere letter to card front.

Apply rub-on transfers to spell 'To My' on tab on card front. Ink edges of a small flower with pink ink; insert a gold brad through flower centre and adhere to tab.

Sponge pink ink onto 'always' flash card; ink edges with brown ink. Attach a rickrack sticker to top edge of flash card. Staple several folded ribbons to right end of flash card. Adhere to first inside panel.

Use black ink to stamp tape measure on ivory card stock; cut out and adhere to the right of 'always' flash card. Use an adhesive dot to adhere a button to tape measure.

Cut off one side of 'laugh' flash card and sponge pink ink onto card; ink edges with brown ink and adhere to centre panel inside card. Adhere vintage plastic sewing tool to top of panel. Ink large flower with brown ink and insert pewter brad through centre; adhere to sewing tool with adhesive dots.

Attach a rickrack sticker to tab on back panel. Cut off one side of 'friend' flash card and sponge on pink ink. Ink edges with brown ink. Adhere to right side of back panel. Use a computer to generate, or hand-print, a large bracket on white paper; print and cut out. Adhere to left side of 'friend' flash card. Insert gold brads through three small flowers; adhere below 'friend.'

Punch a 1⅛-inch circle from printed paper. Apply 'A' rub-on transfer to printed paper; cut out and use foam tape to adhere 'A' to paper circle. Adhere above 'friend' with foam tape.

Cut a 1¼-inch square from printed paper; use a craft knife to cut out a ½-inch-square opening, forming a square frame. Use a computer to generate, or hand-print, 'be' on ivory card stock; cut a small rectangle around word to fit frame. Adhere rectangle to back of frame; adhere to top of back panel. Adhere chipboard ampersand beside frame. ■

SOURCES: Printed papers and 'A' rub-on transfer from BasicGrey; 'F' monogram from Three Bugs in a Rug; flash cards from 7gypsies; chipboard ampersand from Heidi Swapp/ Advantus Corp.; rubber stamp from Stampington & Co.

Sorry I've Been a Witch

Let this whimsical witch deliver your heart-felt apology with a smile.

DESIGN BY DEBRA REYNOLDS

Materials

Card stock: purple, green
Printed papers: green floral, lavender striped
Witch sticker
Black dye ink pad
Black fine-tip marker
Black rub-on transfers: alphabet, 2 small flowers
3/8-inch-wide orange polka-dot grosgrain ribbon
Stapler with staples
Distressing tool
Glue stick

Form a 4¼ x 5½-inch side-folded card from purple card stock. Cut a 4 x 3-inch piece of green floral printed paper; ink edges and adhere to top half of card as shown. Cut a 4 x 2-inch piece of green card stock; ink edges and adhere to bottom half of card as shown. Cut a 4 x 1½-inch piece of lavender striped paper; ink edges and adhere to card as shown.

Cut a 2½ x 4-inch rectangle from purple card stock; distress edges. Ink rectangle. Attach witch sticker to rectangle. Cut three 1-inch lengths of ribbon; fold each in half and staple two to upper left corner of rectangle and one to lower right corner. Adhere to card front. Apply rub-on transfers to card to spell 'sorry'; apply flowers to each side of word.

For inside, cut a 4 x 5¼-inch piece of green card stock; ink rectangle. Adhere to right inside flap of card. Apply rub-on transfers inside card to spell 'witch!'; hand-print 'so sorry that I've been such a' above word and 'please forgive me?!' below word. ∎

SOURCES: Printed paper from Provo Craft; sticker from SEI; rub-on transfers from Doodlebug Design Inc.

Crabby

Need to apologize for some grumpy behaviour? A bit of sand and some tiny shells add authenticity.

DESIGN BY ALICE GOLDEN

Materials
Pale blue card stock
Ivory scallop-edge envelope to fit a 4¼ x 5½-inch card
Rubber stamps: crab, 'Sorry I've Been Crabby'
Dark green fine-detail pigment ink pad
Small amount of sand
Mini shells
Distressing tool
Clear-drying liquid glue

Form a 4¼ x 5½-inch side-folded card from pale blue card stock; distress right edge of card front. Stamp crab on card as shown. Apply a small amount of glue below crab and sprinkle on sand; let dry. Adhere shells to card as shown; let dry. Stamp sentiment inside card. Stamp crab on envelope as desired. ■

SOURCES: Rubber stamps from Rubber Soul; distressing tool from Making Memories; scallop-edged envelope from K&Company; ink pad from Tsukineko Inc.

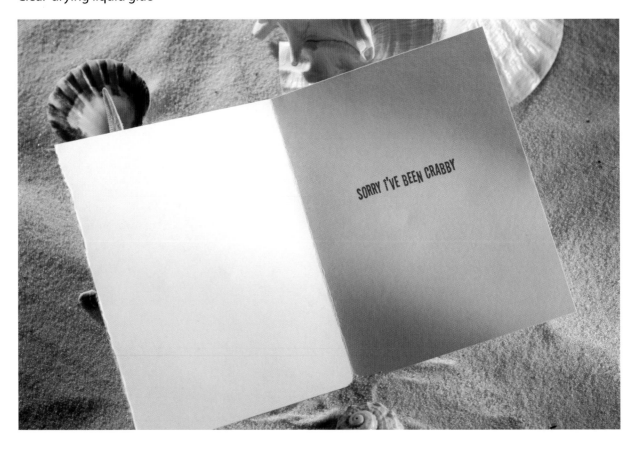

Have a Magical Day

Sometimes you need a little magic fairy dust to get you through the day!

DESIGN BY JULIE EBERSOLE

Materials
4¼-inch-square pink note card with envelope
Card stock: pink printed, pale pink
Rubber stamps: fairy, 'have a MAGICAL day,' wand, decorative oval, stars
Chalk ink pads: dark brown, pink
2 small rhinestone star stickers
2 pink ribbons
Watercolour pencils
Blender pen
Fine glitter
Decorative-edge scissors
Adhesive foam dots
Glue pen
Glue stick

Stamp 'have a MAGICAL day' and a fairy on a 2⅝ x 2-inch piece of pink printed card stock with dark brown ink; colour fairy with watercolour pencils, using blender pen to blend colours as desired. Let dry. Attach star sticker above 'I' in 'MAGICAL.' Use glue pen to apply glitter to image as desired. Adhere to pale pink card stock; trim edges with decorative-edge scissors. Use foam dots to adhere assembled panel to card. Wrap ribbons through card and knot on front; trim ribbon ends.

Decorate envelope with stamps and remaining star sticker. ■

SOURCES: Note card, card stock, twinkle star stickers and rubber stamps from A Muse Artstamps; chalk ink from Clearsnap Inc.; blender pen from Uchida of America; glue pen from Sakura of America.

have a MAGICAL day

File Folder Birthday Wishes

A mini file folder filled with a trio of wishes adorns this easy-to-make card.

DESIGN BY LORETTA MATEIK

Materials
Printed card stock: Weathered Nutmeg,
  Weathered White, Wheat Field
White envelope to fit a 4¼ x 5½-inch card
Birthday-themed words rub-on transfers
Stickers: 'Happy Birthday,' embossed 'Birthday'
  and 'Wishes'
Dye ink pads: light brown, black
⅜-inch-wide brown with white stitches ribbon
Metal spiral clip
Sandpaper
Round sponge dauber
Stiff brush
Stapler with staples
Double-sided tape
Glue stick

Form a 4¼ x 5½-inch side-folded card from Weathered Nutmeg card stock; lightly sand. Cut 'Happy Birthday' sticker in half and attach each word to Weathered White card stock; cut a rectangle around each word; ink edges with light brown ink and adhere to card as shown.

Use provided pattern to trace and cut a mini file folder from Wheat Field card stock; score and fold on dashed line. Rub light brown ink across folder; attach 'Birthday' and 'Wishes' stickers to folder. Apply desired birthday word rub-on transfers to Weathered White card stock; trim rectangles around words to fit inside folder. Staple folded ribbon pieces to ends of rectangles; insert rectangles inside folder and close with clip. Adhere folder to card with double-sided tape.

Apply black ink onto stiff brush and lightly brush ink across envelope; repeat as desired. Ink round sponge dauber with light brown ink; stamp circles on left side of envelope. ∎

SOURCES: Printed card stock from Lasting Impressions for Paper Inc.; embossed stickers from K&Company; rub-on transfers from Royal & Langnickel.

File Folder Birthday Wishes
Score and fold on dashed line

A Day of Adventure

Distressed edges add dimension to a card that's perfectly suited for kids.

DESIGN BY ERIN BIGLER

Materials
Chili card stock
Danny O printed paper: Ransom Words, blue
Small chipboard letters: H, B
Walnut distress ink
Sponge
Letter stickers
Assorted buttons
Blue twill tape
Black-and-white gingham ribbon
Distresser tool
Adhesive dots or glue

Cut a piece of chili card stock 9 x 5¾ inches; fold in half to make a side-fold card 4½ x 5¾ inches. Roughen edges with distresser tool.

Cover top half of card front with blue printed paper and bottom half with Ransom Words printed paper. Cover seam between the two with a length of blue twill tape.

Sponge chipboard letters H and B with walnut distress ink. Attach to card with letter stickers to spell 'Happy Birthday.'

Attach buttons to twill tape as desired. Tie a short length of gingham ribbon through a knot in a length of blue twill tape; attach to centre button. ■

SOURCES: Danny O printed paper from K&Company; small chipboard letters from We R Memory Keepers; letter stickers from Doodlebug Design Inc.; distress ink from Ranger Industries Inc.

Happy Birthday

Add a little glitz with a rhinestone brad for an elegantly simple card.

DESIGN BY KATE THAETE

Materials
Card stock: white, sage green
Rubber stamps: flower, 'HAPPY,' 'Birthday'
Sage green dye ink pad
Watercolour brush
Watercolours
Rhinestone brad
⅜-inch-wide sage green ribbon
Hole punches: ¹⁄₁₆- and ⅛-inch
Sewing machine with white thread
Glue stick

Form a 4¼ x 5½-inch top-folded card from white card stock. Cut a 6 x 2¼-inch rectangle from sage green card stock; stamp repeatedly with flowers. Place rectangle on card ⅝ inch from top, aligning left edges. Fold up excess on right side and tear off end, leaving a 1½-inch flap. Remove from card and machine-stitch flap in place as shown. Stamp 'HAPPY' five times on flap. Adhere to card as shown.

Stamp a flower onto white card stock; cut a 2¼ x 2-inch rectangle around flower. Watercolour flower; let dry. Adhere to card as shown. Punch a ¹⁄₁₆-inch hole through flower centre; insert brad.

Cut a ½ x 1⅜-inch rectangle from sage green card stock; cut off top corners, forming a tag. Punch a ⅛-inch hole through top of tag. Stamp 'Birthday' onto tag. Wrap ribbon twice around bottom half of card; put one end of ribbon through hole in tag and tie tag in place; trim ribbon ends. ■

SOURCES: Flower rubber stamp from Stampin' Up!; word rubber stamps and rhinestone brad from Making Memories.

HAPPY
HAPPY
HAPPY
HAPPY
HAPPY

Birthday

Birthday Balloons

A dimensional sticker is the focus of this super-simple birthday card.

DESIGN BY KATHLEEN PANEITZ

Materials
Matchbook-style card
Lavender plaid paper
Balloons printed glitter vellum
Friendship quotation
Dimensional balloons glitter sticker
'Happy Birthday' jelly label
⅝-inch-wide green polka-dot grosgrain ribbon
ENV-1 envelope template
2-fold fastener
2 fabric reinforcements
⅛-inch hole punch
Instant-dry paper adhesive

Adhere lavender plaid paper to bottom card panel; trim edges even. Adhere friendship quotation to lower right corner. Attach balloons sticker to left side.

Punch two ⅛-inch holes through top card panel approximately 2½ inches apart; adhere fabric reinforcements over holes. Attach fastener through holes. Attach jelly label to top panel. Tie ribbon in a bow and adhere above quotation.

Use template to trace and cut an envelope from glitter vellum; assemble envelope. ∎

SOURCES: Printed papers from Sweetwater; friendship quotation and matchbook-style card from Die Cuts With A View; jelly label from Making Memories; fastener from Magic Scraps; dimensional sticker and glitter vellum from K&Company; fabric reinforcements from 7 gypsies; envelope template from The C-Thru Ruler Co.; paper adhesive from Beacon Adhesives Inc.

[HAPPY BIRTHDAY]

MANY PEOPLE WILL
WALK IN AND OUT OF
YOUR LIFE, BUT ONLY
True friends
WILL LEAVE FOOTPRINTS
IN YOUR HEART.

ELEANOR ROOSEVELT

Reach for the Stars

Celebrate your loved one's accomplishment with a multi-fold tag card.

DESIGN BY SUSAN STRINGFELLOW

Materials
Assorted double-sided printed card stocks from Love Notes collection
Black fine-tip marker
Chipboard star
Decorative motif rubber stamp
Black dye ink pad
Alphabet template (optional)
Assorted fibres and ribbons
Orange/silver brad
Sandpaper
#TPL01 A2 envelope template
Punches: ³⁄₁₆-inch hole, star
4 orange eyelets with eyelet-setting tool
Removable adhesive
Paper adhesive
Computer and printer
Computer paper

Cut a 10¾ x 5¼-inch piece of printed card stock. Use a computer to generate three lines of 'Congrats' vertically on computer paper. Attach card-stock piece on top of printed words with removable adhesive and run through printer again. *Option: Hand-print words along one long side of card-stock piece with black marker.* Accordion-fold card stock into four equal sections, each measuring approximately 2¹¹⁄₁₆ x 5¼ inches; while folded, cut off upper corners diagonally, forming a tag-shaped card. Ink edges.

Punch a ³⁄₁₆-inch hole through centre top of each section; set eyelets. Tie fibres or ribbons through eyelets. Stamp decorative motifs along bottom edge.

Use a computer to generate 'grad,' leaving space between letters and sizing each letter to be approximately two to three inches tall; print letters in reverse on the reverse side of printed card stock. *Option: Use alphabet template in place of a computer.* Cut out letters; ink edges and adhere one to each panel.

Use chipboard star as a template to cut a star from printed card stock; adhere card stock to star. Sand and ink edges. Punch a star from contrasting printed card stock; ink edges and adhere to chipboard star. Write 'reach for the stars' along star border. Use brad to attach star to lower left corner on card front (panel with 'g').

Use envelope template to cut an envelope from printed card stock; ink edges. Assemble envelope. Punch a star from contrasting printed card stock; ink edges and adhere to top flap. ■

SOURCES: Printed card stock from Cosmo Cricket Inc.; rubber stamp from Sugarloaf Products Inc.; chipboard star from Deluxe Designs; brad from SEI; envelope template from JudiKins Inc.

Celebrate, Wish, Dream

A dramatic black-and-white card celebrates a momentous occasion.

DESIGN BY LINDA BEESON

Materials

Card stock: white, black
Printed papers: gray grid, gray polka-dot
White rub-on transfers: graduation-themed words, alphabet
Black 'dare to DREAM' rub-on transfer
Black dye ink pad
3 pewter round snaps
Purchased envelope template, or template on page 154
⅛-inch hole punch
Glue stick

Form a 4¾ x 6-inch top-folded card from white card stock. Form a 4½ x 6-inch top-folded card from gray grid printed paper; ink edges. Place printed paper card centred across fold of white card and adhere. Cut a 3⅝ x 5¼-inch piece of gray polka-dot printed paper; ink edges and adhere to card near right edge.

Using white rub-on transfers, apply 'GRAD' toward centre of a 3⅞ x 2¼-inch piece of black card stock; apply desired graduation-themed words until card-stock piece is covered. Adhere to card as shown. Punch three ⅛-inch holes, evenly spaced, through lower right side of card front. Attach snaps.

Form envelope from gray grid printed paper using purchased template, or template from page 154. Apply 'dare to DREAM' rub-on transfer to lower right corner of envelope front. ■

SOURCES: Printed papers from BasicGrey; rub-on transfers from Making Memories and DMD Inc.; snaps from Making Memories; envelope template from Printworks Collection Inc.

You Did It!

This simple card is well-suited to celebrating any special accomplishment.

DESIGN BY RANDI LANZ

Materials
Blue pocket card with tag insert and envelope
Green plaid printed paper
Graduation-themed vellum quotation
5 white/green mosaic tiles
Black rub-on transfers: 'You did it …,' 'congrats!'
¼-inch-wide bright green ribbon
Bright green fibres
Paper flower
Yellow mini round brad
¹⁄₁₆-inch hole punch
Adhesive dots
Adhesive applicator with permanent adhesive cartridges

Using rub-on transfers, apply 'You did it … congrats!' to lower right side on front of pocket card, leaving room below sentiment for mosaic tiles. Use adhesive dots to adhere mosaic tiles below sentiment.

Adhere a 4¼-inch length of ribbon along front flap of pocket. Punch a ¹⁄₁₆-inch hole through flower centre; insert brad. Adhere flower to right side of front flap over ribbon.

Cut a 4½ x 6-inch piece of green plaid printed paper; tear off upper left corner. Referring to photo, adhere paper to tag, leaving upper left portion empty. Trim edges even with tag. Adhere vellum quotation to tag. Adhere a 3¾-inch length of ribbon to tag ½ inch above bottom edge. Tie a bow with another piece of ribbon; trim ends and adhere to right side of ribbon on tag. Tie fibres onto tag. Insert tag inside pocket card. ■

SOURCES: Pocket card with tag and rub-on transfers from Making Memories; printed paper and vellum quotation from Die Cuts With A View; mosaic tiles from Sarah Heidt Photo Craft; adhesive applicator and cartridges from Xyron.

And the day came
when the risk
it took to remain
tight inside the bud
was more painful
than the risk it took
to blossom.

~ Nin

You *did* it...
congrats!

Love Labels

Love is defined on this quick and easy card.

DESIGN BY MEREDITH HOLMAN

Materials
4¼ x 5½-inch ivory flecked card with envelope
Brown patterned paper
Pink satin cord
Assorted word stickers
Brown ink pad
Pink brad
Photo anchor
⅛-inch hole punch
Sandpaper
Glue stick

Trim a 4 x 5¼-inch piece of brown patterned paper; ink edges. Sand a word sticker and attach it toward bottom of brown paper. Wrap pink cord around left side of paper twice and tie a knot in front. Glue to card.

Sand four additional word stickers and attach to card, overlapping pink cord. Punch a ⅛-inch hole toward upper right corner of card; attach photo anchor with pink brad.

Ink edges of envelope. Cut a piece of brown patterned paper to fit on reverse side of envelope; adhere. Sand a word sticker; layer onto brown patterned paper. Sand edges and glue to envelope flap. ■

SOURCES: Patterned paper and word stickers from Pebbles Inc.; photo anchor and brad from Making Memories.

He Asked Me!

Announce your engagement with a whimsical, kid-style expression of love.

DESIGN BY TAMI MAYBERRY

Materials

Light green card stock
Green floral and purple patterned papers
Pre-coloured cutouts: girl with flower, flower and frame
Black alphabet rub-on transfers
Black ink pad
Envelope to fit a 5⅞ x 7¾-inch card
Stylus
Glue stick

Cut an 11¾ x 7¾-inch rectangle from light green card stock; score and fold in half. Ink edges of cutouts. Glue frame to card at a slight angle; glue girl with flower frame overlapping first frame. Transfer 'He Asked Me!' to lower right corner of card.

Carefully take apart premade envelope and use as a template to trace and cut an envelope from green floral print paper; score and fold lines. Glue side and bottom flaps together.

Cut a 6 x 4-inch rectangle from purple patterned paper; ink edges. Glue to envelope. Glue flower cutout in lower left corner. ■

SOURCES: Pre-coloured cutouts and patterned papers from Provo Craft; rub-on transfers from Making Memories.

Bridal Shower

DESIGN BY GRETCHEN SCHMIDT

Materials

White and yellow card stock
Yellow floral-print paper
Embellished wedding
   dress sticker

Computer font (optional)
Glue stick

Score and fold an 8½ x 5½-inch piece of white card stock in half forming a 4¼ x 5½-inch card. Layer a 4 x 5¼-inch piece of floral-print paper on top of a 4⅛ x 5⅜-inch piece of yellow card stock; glue to card. Cut a 3⅛ x 1⅛-inch strip of yellow card stock; glue at bottom of card. Hand-print, or use a computer to generate, 'Bridal Shower' on white card stock; trim a rectangle around words and glue on top of yellow card stock strip. Attach wedding dress sticker to card. ■

SOURCES: Floral-print paper from Creative Imaginations; sticker from EK Success.

Memories

DESIGN BY GRETCHEN SCHMIDT

Materials

Pale green and light green card stock
Memory-themed sentiment
White envelope to fit a 5½ x 4¼-inch card
Small key charm
³⁄₁₆-inch-wide off-white picot ribbon
Off-white thread
Key sticker or gold and light green markers
⅛-inch hole punch
Adhesive foam dots
Glue stick

Cut a 5½ x 8½-inch piece of pale green card stock; score and fold in half. Adhere sentiment onto light green card stock; trim a small border. Punch a ⅛-inch hole on left side of layered sentiment.

Thread ribbon through hole; tie a bow and trim ends. String key charm onto off-white thread; tie onto bow. Trim thread ends. Glue assembled piece to card at an angle.

Embellish lower left corner of envelope by drawing a key and bow with markers or attaching a key sticker. ■

SOURCES: Sentiment from My Mind's Eye Inc.

We're Moving

A pocket card made with bubble wrap is the ideal way to announce your move. Tuck a card inside with your new address information.

DESIGN BY MARY LYNN MALONEY

Materials

5 x 7-inch cardboard
Photos
Green card stock
Blue mulberry paper
Plain white paper
Large manila tag
Bubble wrap
Alphabet stamps
Red ink pad
Fine hemp twine
Craft knife
Brown packing tape
Glue stick
Computer and printer

Cut 5 x 7-inch piece of bubble wrap; trim off one upper corner at an angle to create pocket. Affix bubble wrap to front of cardboard with brown packing tape along side and bottom edges, smoothing edges of tape onto back.

Stamp 'We Are Moving' on blue mulberry paper to fit within an area approximately 2 x ⅝ inch. Trim around lettering. Centre and adhere lettering to 4¼ x 1½-inch strip of green card stock; tear card stock along long edges. Adhere card stock across bottom of pocket with glue stick; adhere additional packing tape over the corners.

Tag: Stamp 'Our New Address' at top of tag. Tear bottom edge off tag. Cut and tear 3½ x 2½-inch piece of blue mulberry paper; adhere to tag. Cut and tear a 3 x 1½-inch piece of green card stock; adhere to blue mulberry paper.

Use computer to generate, or hand-print, name and new address on white paper; trim to fit on green card stock; adhere with glue stick.

Affix brown packing tape over the right edge of tag, overlapping address panel. Thread hemp twine through hole in tag.

Slip photos of new home into pocket behind bubble wrap. Slip address tag behind photos. ■

WE ARE MOVING

OUR NEW ADDRESS

The Bakers
1234 Cedar Lane
Pretty Town, US 56789

Home At Last

Send a quick card to friends and family to announce your new roosting place.

DESIGN BY DEE GALLIMORE-PERRY

Materials

Card stock: yellow, white
Midnight Paisley double-sided printed paper
3⅝ x 4⅝-inch birdhouse photo
97% Complete 'Quotes' sticker sheet (includes 'HOME' sticker)
Purchased envelope template, or template on page 154
2 yellow chipboard stars
¼-inch-wide yellow decorative ribbon
Decorative clip
Black fine-tip marker
Sandpaper
Stapler with staples
Paper adhesive
Computer and printer (optional)

Form a 4½ x 6-inch side-folded card from yellow card stock. Sand and distress edges. Sand edges of photo; adhere to non-paisley side of Midnight Paisley printed paper; trim a small border, sand edges and adhere to card front. Staple photo edges as desired.

Attach 'HOME' sticker to lower right edge of card as shown. Sand edges of chipboard stars; staple one to card front as shown. Cut a 4 x 5½-inch piece of Midnight Paisley printed paper; sand edges on non-paisley side and adhere to left inside panel. Tie ribbon to clip; trim ribbon ends. Attach clip to right side of card front.

Hand-print, or use a computer to generate, new address information on white card stock. Cut a 3¾ x 5¼-inch rectangle around words and adhere to non-paisley side of a 4 x 5½-inch piece of Midnight Paisley printed paper. Sand edges. Adhere to inside right panel.

Form envelope from yellow card stock using purchased template or template from page 154. Sand edges. Cut a 1⅜-inch square from Midnight Paisley printed paper; sand edges on non-paisley side. Staple remaining chipboard star to paper square. Adhere to envelope flap. ■

SOURCES: Printed paper from Bo-Bunny Press; clip and sticker sheet from 7gypsies; chipboard stars from Making Memories; ribbon from AMM.

We've Moved!

Please join us for an
Open House Celebration!

Date: August 1, 2007
Time: 2:00 PM

At our new address:
Eddie and Mary Bluebird
222 Chickadee Lane
Newtown, ST 03222

Our Family Grew

A cherished baby photo provides the focal point for this sweet birth announcement.

DESIGN BY MOU SAHA

Materials

6½ x 5-inch white card with envelope
Two-sided blue/polka-dot printed paper
White tissue paper
Approximately 4¾ x 4-inch tinted baby photo*
Metal-edge round vellum tag
Date stamp with letters
Baby footprints rubber stamp
Ink pads: gray antique-finish, brown dye
Fine-tip pens: dark blue, brown

⅝-inch-wide white printed ribbon
Sandpaper
'Miracle' word bead
Paper towel
Blue embroidery floss
Sewing needle
Adhesive dots
Double-sided tape

*Photo can either be tinted by hand with photo-tinting pencils or, if using a digital photo, increase the degree of blue or red with the 'Colour Variation' of any photo-editing software.

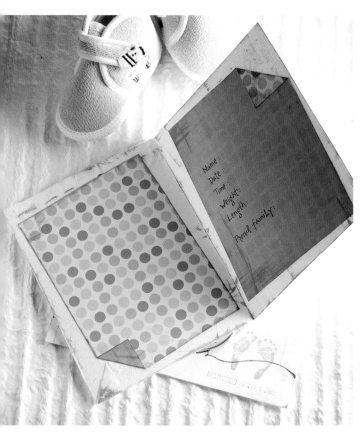

Gently sand edges of photo. Wipe off any dust with paper towel. Centre and adhere photo to card front. Cut a piece of tissue paper approximately 7 x 9 inches. Gently crumple and then smooth out paper. Place paper on top of photo and begin to wrap paper around the card edges and secure with double-sided tape. Gently tear centre of tissue paper, partially exposing photo. Fold tissue edges underneath themselves and secure with double-sided tape.

Lightly rub gray ink pad along edges and surface of card. Thread sewing needle with blue embroidery floss and straight-stitch along right edge of card front, sliding 'Miracle' bead onto centre of thread and proceeding to stitch along remaining right side of card front.

Using brown ink and date stamp, stamp baby's birth date toward top of metal-edge tag; let ink dry slightly and then gently smudge to soften the look. In the remaining space, write 'On (stamped date), our family grew by two feet' with blue pen. Tie ribbon onto tag; trim ribbon ends. Use adhesive

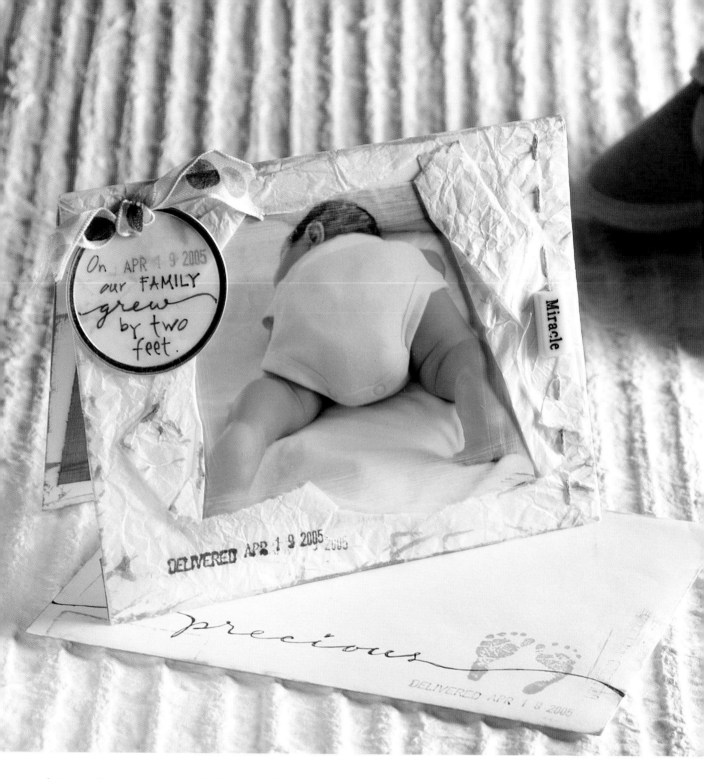

dots to adhere tag to upper left corner of card front. Stamp 'DELIVERED' and birth date on lower left corner of card.

Cut two 5¾ x 4½-inch rectangles from printed paper; ink edges with gray ink. Write desired birth information on blue side of one rectangle. Fold one corner on each rectangle to reveal reverse sides and adhere inside card.

Ink edges of envelope with gray ink. Use gray ink to stamp baby footprints on lower right corner on envelope front and on top envelope flap. Use brown ink to stamp 'DELIVERED' and birth date on lower right corner of envelope front. Write 'precious' across bottom of envelope with brown pen as desired. ■

SOURCES: Printed paper from Keeping Memories Alive; word bead from Hirschberg Schutz & Co. Inc.; rubber stamp from Stampcraft; antique-finish ink pad from Ranger Industries Inc.

Ultrasound Announcement

Give friends and family a sneak peek at the long-awaited arrival.

DESIGN BY TAMI MAYBERRY

Here's a little peek at me, it shows I'm on my way,
Little boys like me don't just happen everyday.
I'm busy growing strong, and one day soon we'll meet,
I can't wait to hug and kiss, the moment will be sweet.
For now dream of me, and all the things we'll do,
Explore, sing, laugh and play, to name a very few.
Save a special place for me to grow inside your heart,
we will be forever friends, a love that never parts.
I hope you'll share your joy, with friends both new and old,
a little boy to love, will soon be yours to hold!

Materials

Card stock: blue, light blue
Printed papers: light blue, blue striped
Ultrasound image
Ultrasound poem*
Black fine-tip marker
Blue dye ink pad
'It's A BOY' rub-on transfer
Baby-themed metal plaque
7½ inches ⅜-inch-wide blue 'It's a Boy!'
   satin ribbon
Purchased envelope template, or template on
   page 155
Paper adhesive
Computer and printer

*Ultrasound poem on sample is from Two Peas in a Bucket and was written by Teri Harrison. It can be found at www.twopeasinabucket.com/peasoup_main.asp?cmd= display&word_id=31187

Adhere a 4¾ x 6⅝-inch piece of light blue printed paper to blue card stock; trim a small border. Form a 3½-inch-square top-folded card from blue card stock; centre and adhere to top of layered rectangle. Apply 'It's A BOY' rub-on transfer and adhere metal plaque to card as shown. Trim ultrasound image to fit inside card; adhere to card.

Hand-print, or use a computer to generate, ultrasound poem on light blue card stock. Cut a rectangle around words; ink edges and adhere to bottom of panel.

Form envelope from blue striped paper using purchased template or template from page 155. Adhere ribbon to bottom of envelope at an angle; trim edges even. ■

SOURCES: Printed papers from Provo Craft and Doodlebug Design Inc.; rub-on transfer and metal plaque from Making Memories; envelope template from Provo Craft/Coluzzle.

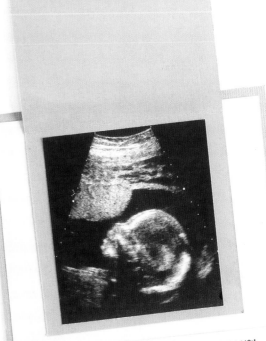

Here's a little peek at me, it shows I'm on my way,
Little boys like me don't just happen everyday.
I'm busy growing strong, and one day soon we'll meet,
I can't wait to hug and kiss, the moment will be sweet.
For now dream of me, and all the things we'll do,
Explore, sing, laugh and play, to name a very few.
Save a special place for me to grow inside your heart,
we will be forever friends, a love that never parts.
I hope you'll share your joy, with friends both new and old,
a little boy to love, will soon be yours to hold!

It's a Girl

A black-and-white photo framed in handmade paper makes an adorable birth announcement.

DESIGN BY ANGIE HAGIST

Materials
4 x 4⅞-inch side-folded blank card
Darling Diva handmade papers: white, pink
Approximately 3¾ x 2½-inch black-and-white baby photo
Black and pink fine-tip markers
Die-cutting machine with small heart die
Paper glue
Computer and printer (optional)

Project note: *Some computer fonts may not print well on handmade paper; experiment with different fonts to find one that does.*

Hand-print, or use a computer to generate, desired greeting and announcement information onto shiny side of pink handmade paper; cut a 3¾ x 4½-inch rectangle around words, positioning words on centre bottom of rectangle.

Cut a piece of white handmade paper to fit card front; adhere paper to card with shiny side face up. Centre and adhere pink rectangle to card. Adhere photo to card as shown.

Die-cut six hearts from pink handmade paper; adhere to upper left corner of card as shown. Trim card edges if needed. ∎

SOURCES: Handmade papers from Paper Tapestry; die-cutting machine and die from Ellison/Sizzix.

It's A Girl
Delaney Alexis Hagise
January 2, 2006
6 lbs. 15 oz.

Baby Confetti Cards

Celebrate a new arrival with confetti-packed cards.

DESIGN BY BARBARA GREVE

Materials

Card stock: pink, blue
Printed papers: pink gingham, baby boy–
   themed words, blue striped
Tissue papers: light pink, white
White vellum
Newsprint
Plastic wrap
Envelopes to fit 6½ x 5-inch cards
Baby-themed sentiments rub-on transfers
Baby-themed confetti
Ribbon or fibre: light pink or blue
Rickrack: light pink or blue
Metal-edge round tag
Silver heart snap
Cutting tool with rectangle and square templates
Hole punches: ¼- and ⅛-inch
Decorative-edge scissors
Foam brush
Craft knife
Vellum tape
Spray adhesive
Gem glue
Fabric glue

Confetti Paper: Lay an 8½ x 11-inch piece of plastic wrap flat on work surface; sprinkle confetti as desired on plastic wrap. If making confetti paper for a girl, add torn strips of light pink tissue paper. Cover the confetti with a sheet of white tissue paper.

Mix gem glue with water until it reaches a cream-like consistency. Brush the glue mixture onto the back of the tissue paper, making sure it is well-saturated through to the plastic wrap, but making sure to not tear the tissue paper. Let dry. Carefully

peel the tissue paper off of the plastic wrap and the confetti will remain on the tissue paper.

Baby Girl Card: Cut a 6½ x 10-inch piece of pink card stock; score and fold in half. Use cutting tool and square template to cut three 1½-inch squares, evenly spaced, along bottom edge of card.

Cut a 6½ x 4½-inch piece of pink gingham printed paper. In the same manner as above, cut 2-inch squares, equally spaced, near bottom edge of paper. Trim bottom edge with decorative-edge scissors. Use fabric glue to adhere paper to card front, positioning cut-out squares on top of the cut-out squares on card. Adhere light pink rickrack to top edge of pink gingham printed paper on card.

Cut out three pieces from confetti paper to fit behind square openings. Use fabric glue to adhere confetti paper squares to reverse sides of openings. Glue a piece of white card stock to the backs of the confetti paper squares.

Transfer a baby-themed sentiment to vellum; cut a rectangle around sentiment. Adhere to pink card stock; trim a ⅛-inch border, trimming bottom edge with decorative-edge scissors. Adhere assembled panel to card centred above middle square. Tie a bow with pink ribbon; centre and glue below assembled panel. Trim ribbon ends.

Baby Boy Card: Cut a 10 x 6½-inch piece of blue card stock; score and fold in half. Cut a 4¾ x 3-inch piece of baby boy–themed words print paper with 'baby boy' positioned along top edge. Trim bottom edge with decorative-edge scissors. Adhere to card front near top edge. Adhere blue rickrack to top edge of baby boy-themed words printed paper.

Cut a 4¾ x 3½-inch piece of vellum; tear off top

edge. Place vellum on newsprint and trace around vellum; use craft knife to cut out traced area on newsprint. Working in a well-ventilated area, cover card front with newsprint, positioning it so that the opening is where the vellum will be placed. Spray opening with adhesive. Arrange confetti on sprayed area of card. Spray back of vellum with adhesive and secure to card, covering confetti.

Use cutting tool and square template to cut a 1¼-inch square from blue striped paper; centre and cut a 1½-inch square around first square, forming a frame. Repeat to make a total of three frames. Place paper frames on top of confetti paper and cut out three squares to fit inside frames. Use fabric glue to adhere papers to frames. Adhere frames, evenly spaced, to top of card.

Cut a circle from blue striped paper to fit round tag; adhere circle to tag. Punch a ¼-inch hole through circle. Punch a ⅛-inch hole through tag

and attach heart snap. Use craft knife to cut a small slit through fold of card 3¾ inches from top; thread blue fibre through slit. Tie tag onto fibre; trim fibre ends.

Envelope: Using cutting tool and rectangle template, cut a 3½ x 2-inch rectangle from pink gingham or blue striped paper. Trim edges with decorative-edge scissors. Cut a 3 x 1½-inch opening inside rectangle, forming a frame. Cut a piece of vellum to fit behind rectangle frame. Adhere confetti to the vellum rectangle and adhere to envelope front. Glue rectangle frame around vellum. Cut a ½-inch-wide strip of co-ordinating paper; trim bottom edge with decorative-edge scissors and adhere to top edge of envelope. ■

SOURCES: Printed papers from Making Memories and Creative Imaginations; rub-on transfers from Making Memories; cutting tool and templates from Fiskars.

Baby Tag Cards

Die-cut tags provide the base for this cute set of baby cards.

DESIGNS BY SHERRY WRIGHT

Materials

Blue or pink printed papers, including polka dots
Stickers: alphabet, 'daughter' or 'son'
Die cuts: large tag, 'received' tag, circles
Fine-tip markers: black, white
Blue dye ink pad (for boy)
Flowers: paper, silk
Blue button (for boy)
Chipboard or plastic 'B'
Blue or pink ribbons
Pink rickrack (for girl)
Brads
Punches: ¹⁄₁₆-inch hole, 1¼-inch circle
Paper adhesive

Decorate top half of large tag die cut with circle die cuts, ribbon or rickrack, printed paper strips and flowers. Embellish plastic or chipboard 'B' as desired with ink, white marker and/or printed paper; adhere to tag as shown. Attach alphabet stickers beside 'B' to complete the word 'Baby.' Tie ribbons through hole on card; trim ribbon ends.

Decorate back of tag with rickrack or printed paper. Tie ribbon onto 'received' tag die cut; trim ribbon ends and adhere to card. Write birth announcement information on sticker with black marker. Attach alphabet stickers to tag to spell baby's name.

Enlarge provided pattern (page 153), and trace and cut an envelope from polka-dots printed paper; assemble envelope. Attach 'daughter' or 'son' sticker to front of envelope; punch a 1¼-inch circle from printed paper and adhere to one end of sticker. Adhere a flower to circle. ■

SOURCES: Die cuts and alphabet stickers from Daisy D's Paper Co.; plastic letter from Heidi Swapp/Advantus Corp.; chipboard letter from Making Memories; flowers from Doodlebug Design Inc.; paper adhesive from Beacon Adhesives Inc.

Floral Sympathy

Send your condolences in this elegant card of muted browns.

DESIGN BY LISA JOHNSON

Materials
2 (4¼ x 4¼-inch) brown note cards with envelope
White card stock
Rubber stamps: flower and vine background, 'In sympathy'
Ink pads: brown chalk, red dye
Aged copper label holder
³⁄₁₆-inch-wide brown stitched ribbon
Craft sponge
Heat tool (optional)
Mini adhesive dots
Glue stick

Cut a 4 x 4-inch rectangle from white card stock; use brown ink to stamp flowers and vine background onto rectangle. Let dry or heat set ink. Centre and adhere to note card with card fold at top.

Use brown ink to stamp 'In sympathy' on white card stock; cut a rectangle around words to fit inside label holder. Adhere rectangle inside label holder.

Cut a 4¼ x ⅝-inch strip from the extra note card. Thread ribbon through holes on label holder and proceed to wrap ribbon around brown strip, positioning label holder in centre of strip. Tie ribbon in a knot on left side. Secure ribbon and label holder with mini adhesive dots. Referring to photo for placement, adhere assembled brown strip to card front ¾ inch above bottom edge.

For envelope, use brown ink to stamp flower and vine background along bottom edge of envelope front. Sponge red ink onto envelope edges. ∎

SOURCES: Note cards and rubber stamps from A Muse Artstamps; chalk ink from Tsukineko Inc.; label holder from Stampin' Up!

Thinking of You

Let them know you care in the difficult times with a card from the heart.

DESIGN BY MELANIE DOUTHIT

Materials
Light brown card stock
Printed papers: tan crosses, brown decorative motif
Cream envelope to fit a 5½ x 4¼-inch card
'Thinking of You' rubber stamp
Brown dye ink pad
⅜-inch-wide light brown grosgrain ribbon
Cross charm
Punches: rounded corner, ⅛-inch hole
Mini adhesive dots
Glue stick

Cut a 5½ x 8½-inch piece of light brown card stock; score and fold in half, forming a 5½ x 4¼-inch card. Ink edges. Cut a 1⅝ x 4-inch rectangle from tan crosses printed paper; round corners with punch. Ink edges and adhere to left side of card front.

Cut a 3⅜ x 4-inch piece of brown decorative motif printed paper; round corners with punch and ink edges. Adhere to right side of card front. Stamp 'thinking of you' on solid portion of tan crosses printed paper; cut a rectangle around sentiment. Round corners with punch and ink edges. Adhere to brown decorative motif printed paper on card.

Punch two ⅛-inch holes through lower right corner of sentiment rectangle; tie ribbon through holes and tie on cross charm. Trim ribbon ends diagonally. Secure charm with mini adhesive dots.

Cut a 1-inch-wide piece of brown decorative motif printed paper; adhere to left side of envelope front. ■

SOURCES: Printed papers and charm from Crossed Paths; rubber stamp from Stampin' Up!

With Sympathy

Express your condolences with a handmade card featuring advanced stamping techniques.

DESIGN BY LISA JOHNSON

Materials

Card stock: ivory, tan, dark green
White envelope to fit a 4¼ x 5½-inch card
Rubber stamps: harlequin background, handwriting, flower, flower detail, splatter, 'With Sympathy'
Dye ink pads: sage green, golden yellow, purple
Dye-ink markers: light green, green, golden yellow, purple
Clear glitter
¼-inch-wide light green gingham ribbon
Aged copper clip
Rounded corner punch
Dimensional adhesive dots
Adhesive dots
Clear-drying glue

Project note: *When applying the dye-ink markers to the rubber stamps, begin with the lightest colour to allow colours to blend without bleeding the darker colours into the lighter colours.*

Cut an 8½ x 5½-inch piece of ivory card stock; score and fold in half, forming a 4¼ x 5½-inch card. Using sage green ink, stamp harlequin background onto card front; inking directly to card, rub golden yellow ink onto card front, applying more along the edges.

Cut a 2 x 5-inch rectangle from tan card stock; round the left corners with punch. Ink the handwriting image with golden yellow ink and stamp on rectangle. In the same manner as before, rub golden yellow ink onto rectangle. Adhere to left side of card front with adhesive dots.

Cut a 2⅜ x 3¼-inch rectangle from ivory card stock. Apply the following colours onto the flower stamp with markers: light green on the stem and leaves, golden yellow on the flower and purple on inner areas of flower. Stamp flower onto the ivory rectangle. Apply the following colours onto the flower detail stamp with markers: purple on flower, golden yellow on flower centre and green on stem and leaves. Stamp detail flower on top of first flower. Ink splatter image with purple ink and stamp randomly on rectangle. Round the right corners of rectangle with punch. Ink edges with golden yellow ink. Tie ribbon onto one side of clip; trim ribbon ends. Slide clip onto upper left corner of flower rectangle. Adhere assembled rectangle to dark green card stock with dimensional adhesive dots and trim a narrow border. Apply a small amount of glue to flower centre and sprinkle on glitter; let dry.

Use purple ink to stamp 'With Sympathy' on tan card stock; cut a rectangle around words and round corners with punch. Ink edges with golden yellow ink. Referring to photo for placement, adhere flower and word rectangles to card front with adhesive dots.

For envelope, use sage green ink to stamp harlequin background on right edge of envelope front; rub golden yellow ink on envelope as desired. ∎

SOURCES: Rubber stamps, markers, inks, clip, ribbon, glitter and glue from Stampin' Up!

WITH *Sympathy*

Stitched Thanks

Simple stitching adds dimensional interest to a quick and easy card.

DESIGN BY KIM HUGHES

Materials
White card stock
Printed paper (optional)
Embroidery floss: pink, green
'thanks' circle sticker
Needle
Paper piercer (optional)
Tape
Paper glue (optional)

Cut one 8½ x 5½ piece of white card stock. Fold for a side-fold card.

Lightly transfer flower pattern to front of card using a pencil.

Using a needle or paper piercer, poke holes along your traced lines. Erase the pencil lines. **Note:** *You can also transfer the pattern to the inside of the card so you won't have to erase the pencil lines.*

Use pink embroidery floss for the flower and green embroidery floss for the stem and leaves. Working from back to front, hand-stitch the pattern working the needle through punched holes. Tape loose ends down in back.

If desired, cut printed paper to fit inside front of card and adhere in place.

Adhere circle sticker to centre of flower on front. ■

SOURCES: Duplicates sticker from Pebbles Inc.

**Stitched Thanks
Flower Pattern**

Metal Frame Thank You

A rub-on transfer applied to a small metal frame adds textural interest.

DESIGN BY TAMI MAYBERRY

Materials
Card stock: white, blue
Printed papers: blue floral, blue dots
White envelope to fit a 6 x 4½-inch card
White metal frame
'Thank You' rub-on transfer
3 white round brads
¹⁄₁₆-inch hole punch
Sewing machine with white thread
Double-sided adhesive foam tape
Instant-dry paper adhesive

Form a 6 x 4½-inch top-folded card from white card stock. Cut a panel of blue card stock slightly smaller than card front; adhere a 2¾ x 4⅛-inch piece of blue floral printed paper to left side of panel; machine-sew a zigzag stitch along long edges of floral rectangle. Punch three ¹⁄₁₆-inch holes through lower right corner of card stock; insert brads. Adhere assembled panel to card.

Apply 'Thank You' rub-on transfer to metal frame; use double-sided adhesive foam tape to adhere frame to card.

Use envelope as a template to trace and cut a piece of blue dots printed paper to fit envelope flap; adhere paper to flap. ∎

SOURCES: Printed papers from BasicGrey; metal frame from Pressed Petals; rub-on transfer from Scenic Route Paper Co.; instant-dry paper adhesive from Beacon Adhesives Inc..

Just the Ticket

Ticket-shaped stickers spell out your gratitude in this horizontal card.

DESIGN BY MELONY BRADLEY

Materials

Card stock: white, olive green
Double-sided brown/striped printed paper
#10 business-size envelope
Stickers: alphabet ticket stubs, green alphabet
Rub-on transfers: 'thank you,' 'merci,' alphabet
⅜-inch-wide black gingham ribbon
Brown chalk ink pad
1-inch circle punch
Instant-dry paper glue

Form a 9 x 4-inch top-folded card from white card stock. Cut a piece of printed paper to fit card front; ink edges and adhere to card with striped side faceup. Adhere a 9-inch length of ribbon to card ⅞ inch from top. Knot the centre of a 3-inch length of ribbon and adhere to longer ribbon ½ inch from right edge of card, as shown.

Attach ticket stub stickers to bottom of card to spell 'TICKET'. Cut a 4-inch square from printed paper; with brown side faceup, tear off the lower right corner diagonally; adhere to upper left corner of card. Attach green alphabet stickers to spell 'just' on top of paper.

Punch five 1-inch circles from olive green card stock; ink edges. Set aside one circle to be used on envelope. Apply 'thank you' rub-on transfer to one circle; apply alphabet rub-on transfers to three circles to spell 'the.' Adhere circles to card as shown.

Adhere a 1½ x 4-inch piece of printed paper to left side of envelope with striped side faceup. Adhere remaining circle to bottom of paper; apply 'merci' rub-on transfer to circle. Ink envelope edges. ■

SOURCES: Printed paper from Crate Paper; green alphabet stickers and rub-on transfers from Making Memories; ticket stub stickers from EK Success; chalk ink pad from Clearsnap Inc.; paper glue from Beacon Adhesives Inc.

Stylish Thanks

Wrap a stamped flower in grosgrain ribbon for a sweet and stylish card.

DESIGN BY CHRISTINE TRAVERSA

Materials

Card stock: white, red
White envelope to fit a 5½ x 4¼-inch card
Rubber stamps: floral square, large flower, small flower
Black dye ink pad
Black fine-tip marker (optional)
8 inches ⅜-inch-wide red with white stitches grosgrain ribbon
Red mini round brad
1-inch circle punch
Hole punches: ¼- and ¹⁄₁₆-inch
Adhesive foam squares
Repositionable adhesive
Glue stick
Computer and printer

Cut a 5½ x 8½-inch piece of white card stock; score and fold in half, forming a 5½ x 4¼-inch card. Use a computer to generate, or hand-print, 'thanks' on lower left corner of card front. **Note:** *If using a computer, first print words on computer paper. Use repositionable adhesive to attach card to paper, positioning card on top of printed word. Run through printer again. Carefully remove card from paper.*

Stamp floral square three times on white card stock; cut a 1⅞ x 1⅞-inch square around each. Adhere squares to red card stock; trim a ⅛-inch border on each. Adhere two squares to top area of card. Set aside remaining square.

Stamp large and small flowers on white card stock; cut out flowers, leaving a small white border on each. Punch a ¼-inch hole through centre of large flower. Wrap ribbon around remaining square; place large flower on top of square and thread ribbon ends through centre of flower, from front to back. Trim ribbon ends diagonally.

Punch a ¹⁄₁₆-inch hole through centre of small flower; insert brad. Use a foam square to adhere small flower to centre of large flower, securing ribbon. Referring to photo for placement, use foam squares to adhere assembled square to card front.

Cut a 3⅛ x ⅛-inch piece of red card stock; adhere to lower right side of card front.

For envelope, stamp floral square and small flower on white card stock; cut out, leaving a small white border on each. Punch ¼- and 1-inch circles from red card stock; adhere ¼-inch circle to small flower. Adhere flower to 1-inch circle; adhere circle to floral square image. Adhere assembled square to lower left corner on envelope front. ∎

SOURCES: Rubber stamps from Stampin' Up!

Pocket of Thanks

Express your appreciation with a tag card adorned with potted flowers.

DESIGN BY AMBER CROSBY

Materials
Pocket card with tag insert and envelope
Ivory card stock
Printed paper: ivory handwritten text
Rubber stamps: potted flowers, 'Thanks'
Ink pads: black, brown
Watercolour pencils
Ribbons: 5/16-inch-wide green striped, 1/8-inch-wide green with white stitching, 3/8-inch-wide sage green with white stitching
4 copper mini round brads
Punches: 1/16-inch hole, 2-inch square
1/8-inch-wide double-sided tape
Glue stick
Computer and printer

Using black ink, stamp four flower images onto ivory card stock. Colour flowers with watercolour pencils. Cut out flower images; glue three, evenly spaced, to bottom of card. Set aside remaining flower for envelope.

Using black ink, stamp 'Thanks' on ivory card stock. Cut a rectangle around word and ink edges brown. Cut two 2¾-inch lengths of 1/8-inch-wide green with white stitching ribbon. Fold one length in half and place it on one side of word rectangle. Punch a 1/16-inch hole through ribbon and rectangle; insert brad. Repeat for remaining length of ribbon, attaching it to other side of rectangle. Use double-sided tape to adhere rectangle and ribbon to folded down portion of card.

Ink edges of tag insert with brown ink. Thread green striped ribbon through hole in tag and tie a knot; trim ends. Place tag in card.

To embellish envelope, use double-sided tape to adhere a 4½-inch length of sage green ribbon to envelope 1⅝ inch from bottom edge.

Punch out a 2-inch square from ivory printed paper. Glue remaining coloured flower to centre of square; glue square to right side of envelope, overlapping ribbon.

Use a computer to generate, or hand-print, 'Especially For You' on ivory card stock. Ink edges brown. Punch a 1/16-inch hole at each end; insert brads. Glue toward top of envelope. ■

SOURCES: Pocket card from Making Memories; printed paper from K&Company; rubber stamps from Inkadinkado; ribbons from Making Memories and Li'l Davis Designs.

Red Delicious Treats

This tasty expression of your gratitude will be warmly received.

DESIGN BY DEB REYNOLDS

Materials
Card stock: ivory, red
Apples printed paper
Ivory envelope to fit a 5 x 5¼-inch card
Black letter rub-on transfers
Black dye ink pad
Mounting tabs
Adhesive dots

Cut a 10 x 5¼-inch piece of ivory card stock; score and fold in half, forming a 5 x 5¼-inch card.

Centre and adhere a 4¼ x 4½-inch piece of apples printed paper to red card stock; trim a narrow border. Ink edges. Centre and adhere to card front.

Cut a 5 x 1½-inch piece of ivory card stock; ink edges and adhere to a 5 x 1⅝-inch piece of red card stock. Ink edges. Cut one apple from apples printed paper; adhere to left edge of layered strip; trim edge even. Apply letter rub-on transfers to spell 'thank you' on layered strip. Adhere assembled strip to card front ½ inch from bottom edge. ■

SOURCES: Printed paper from Die Cuts With A View; rub-on transfers from Making Memories.

thank you

Lucky Me

A colour photo of clover is embellished with rubber-stamped words in this clever card.

DESIGN BY SUSAN STRINGFELLOW

Materials
Black card stock
Tan printed paper
Approximately 3⅞ x 5-inch photo of green clovers
Rubber stamps: Wayfarer Lowercase Letters set,
    Functuation set (includes curly bracket and
    an asterisk)
Black pearlescent ink pad
Black fine-tip marker
Sewing machine with tan thread
Glue stick
Computer and AL Messenger computer font
    (optional)

Form a 4¼ x 5½-inch side-folded card from black card stock. Cut a 4⅛ x 5¼-inch piece of tan printed paper; centre and adhere to card front.

Adhere photo to card.

Hand-print, or use a computer to generate, 'Me' on tan printed paper; cut an approximately 1⅛ x ¾-inch shape around word and adhere to lower right area of photo; open card and machine-stitch along top and right edges of 'Me' shape.

Hand-print, or use a computer to generate, 'to have a friend like you' and 'Happy St. Patrick's Day!' on tan printed paper; cut desired shapes around words. Adhere first set of words toward top inside card; adhere remaining set of words to bottom inside card. Machine-stitch along top edges of words.

Stamp '{lucky}' on card front above 'Me'; stamp an asterisk beside 'Me.' Let ink dry. ∎

SOURCES: Printed paper from BasicGrey; rubber stamps from Technique Tuesday; pearlescent ink pad from Jacquard Products.

Luck of the Irish

Non-Irish friends will appreciate it when you send them the gift of luck.

DESIGN BY SUSAN STRINGFELLOW

Materials
Orange card stock
Oh, Baby Girl! printed papers: Sophie, Larkspur, Peapod, Hannah
Black fine-tip marker
⅜-inch-wide ribbon: orange polka dots, green decorative
Green rhinestone brad
Envelope template to fit a 4¼ x 5½-inch card
Punches: ⅛-inch hole, ¾-inch circle
Die-cutting machine with double-heart die
Sewing machine with green thread
Adhesive foam tape
Paper adhesive
Computer and printer (optional)

Form a 4¼ x 5½-inch side-folded card from orange card stock. Cut a piece of Sophie paper slightly smaller than card front; adhere paper to card.

Hand-print, or use a computer to generate, 'May the luck of the irish …' and '… be smilin' upon ye!' on Larkspur paper; cut desired shapes around words. Adhere the first set of words to lower right corner of card.

Cut a 5½-inch length of each ribbon; referring to photo, place ribbons on card and machine-sew a zigzag stitch around perimeter of card and about one inch up from ribbon ends to secure ribbons. Twist ribbons once and secure remaining ribbon ends to card where shamrock centre will be located.

Die-cut four double hearts from Peapod paper; referring to photo, adhere the heart outline shapes to the card in the shape of a flower, applying adhesive to centres only. Punch a ¾-inch circle from Hannah paper; arrange solid heart shapes in a flower shape; place pink circle on flower centre and secure with rhinestone brad. Adhere to card as shown with foam tape.

Cut two small pieces of desired ribbon; place ribbons and remaining sentiment inside card and secure with a zigzag stitch.

Use envelope template to trace and cut an envelope from Peapod paper; assemble envelope. Decorate top envelope flap with printed paper and card stock as desired; machine-sew decorative stitches on envelope as desired. ■

SOURCES: Printed papers from BasicGrey; ribbons from BasicGrey and American Crafts; die-cutting machine and die from Ellison/Sizzix; envelope template from JudiKins Inc.

Blarney Spoken Here

Watch out for leprechauns this St. Patrick's Day.

DESIGN BY MELANIE DOUTHIT

Materials

Card stock: green, light green
Printed papers: Green Houndstooth, Lucky
White envelope to fit a 5½ x 4¼-inch card
Stickers: shamrock, 'Leprechauns' sign, 'Blarney spoken here' oval
⅝-inch-wide green polka dots grosgrain ribbon
Double-sided tape
Glue stick

Form a 5½ x 4¼-inch top-folded card from green card stock. Cut a 5¼ x 4-inch piece of light green card stock; cut a 5¼ x 2⅜-inch piece of Green Houndstooth paper and a 5¼ x 1¼-inch piece of Lucky paper. Referring to photo, adhere papers to light green card stock.

Attach 'Leprechauns' sign and shamrock stickers to left side of panel. Wrap ribbon around panel, covering seam where papers meet; secure with double-sided tape. Attach 'Blarney spoken here' sticker to right side of panel. Adhere assembled panel to card front.

Cut a desired-size piece of Green Houndstooth paper; layer onto light green card stock and adhere to left side of envelope. Cut out a few shamrocks from Lucky paper; adhere to envelope. ■

SOURCES: Printed papers and stickers from Karen Foster Design.

Love Coupons

Redeemable coupons make Valentine's day a whole lot more fun.

DESIGN BY SHERRY WRIGHT

Materials
Card stock: black, red
Printed papers: white with love-theme words, red swirl with Xs and Os
Black library card pocket
Transparency sheet
'LOVE' embellishment
4 silver heart brads
⅞-inch-wide red sheer ribbon
Black fine-tip permanent marker (optional)
Purchased envelope template, or template on page 155
Die-cutting tool with tag die
Label maker with black label tape
Circle punches: ¼-, ⅛- and ¹⁄₁₆-inch
Glue stick
Double-sided tape
Computer and printer

Cut a 10 x 7-inch piece of black card stock; score and fold in half, forming a 5 x 7-inch card. Cut a 4⅞ x 6⅞-inch piece of love words print paper; centre and adhere to card front.

Cut a 5 x 2-inch rectangle from black card stock. Adhere 'LOVE' embellishment to centre of rectangle. Punch a ¹⁄₁₆-inch hole through both ends of rectangle; insert heart brads. Adhere assembled rectangle to card 1 inch from top edge. Cut a 1-inch square from black card stock; adhere to right edge of card 2⅜ inches from bottom; with card closed, punch a ¼-inch hole through square.

For inside card, cut a 2 x 6⅞-inch piece of red swirl print paper; adhere to left side of right panel inside card. Cut a 3½ x 3⅝-inch piece of love words print paper; adhere to front of library pocket. Adhere pocket inside card, overlapping red swirl paper.

Punch a ¹⁄₁₆-inch hole through lower right corner

inside card; insert heart brad. Cut a 1-inch square from red swirl print paper; adhere to reverse side of card, covering brad ends.

Using label maker, make a 'COUPONS' label, and adhere it to left side of red swirl paper beside pocket. Die-cut three or more tags from red card stock. Punch a ⅛-inch hole through centre top of each tag. Tie an 8-inch length of ribbon onto each. Use a computer to generate, or hand-print with a permanent marker, coupons such as one free movie, one free massage, etc. onto transparency. Cut rectangles around words and adhere one to each tag. Insert tags into pocket.

Cut an 18-inch length of ribbon and thread it through holes on card to tie card shut.

Form envelope from black card stock using purchased template or template from page 155.

Use top envelope flap as a template to trace and cut a piece of love words print paper to fit flap; punch a 1⁄16-inch hole through centre bottom of paper. Insert heart brad. Adhere paper to top envelope flap. Cut a 1-inch-wide strip from red swirl print paper long enough to fit across bottom of envelope. Adhere to bottom of envelope on reverse side.

Cut a piece of red swirl print paper to fit envelope front; adhere paper to envelope. Cut a 2½-inch-wide strip of love words print paper long enough to fit on left side of envelope; adhere to envelope. ∎

SOURCES: Printed papers from Carolee's Creations & Co.; 'LOVE' embellishment from me & my BIG ideas; brads from Provo Craft; die-cutting tool and die from Ellison/Sizzix; template from Green Sneakers Inc.

Adore

A large chipboard monogram and a round coaster dominate this super-simple card.

DESIGN BY LINDA BEESON

Materials

Blue card stock
Co-ordinating printed papers, including striped
Brown envelope to fit a 6 x 4½-inch card
'adore' circle cutout
'a' monogram cutout
Alphabet stickers to spell 'adore'
Green decorative ribbon
¼-inch hole punch
Sewing machine with orange thread
Glue stick

Form a 6 x 4½-inch side-folded card from blue card stock. Cut four 1¾–2½ x 4¼-inch-wide strips from printed papers; adhere to card, overlapping each other. Cut a 1¾ x 4½-inch strip of striped paper; fold in half and adhere to card fold, forming a spine. Machine-sew a zigzag stitch along right edge of spine through all layers. Punch two ¼-inch holes through spine; thread ribbon through holes and tie a knot; trim ribbon ends. Adhere circle cutout and 'a' monogram to card.

Decorate envelope with printed papers; attach alphabet stickers to lower left area of envelope to spell 'adore.' ■

SOURCES: Printed papers, circle cutout and 'a' monogram from My Mind's Eye.

Love You

Metal photo corners frame a stamped expression of your everlasting love.

DESIGN BY JULIE HILLIER

Materials
Card stock: white, red
Printed paper: black with white words
Envelope to fit a 4¼ x 4¼-inch square card
Die-cutting tool and photo corner die
Rubber stamps: decorative heart, 'love you!'
Dye ink pads: red, black, brown
⅜-inch-wide black sheer ribbon
Glue stick

Cut an 8½ x 4¼-inch piece of white card stock; score and fold in half, forming a 4¼ x 4¼-inch square card. Cut a 3⅞ x 3⅞-inch square piece of black/white print paper; adhere to red card stock. Trim a narrow border. Adhere to card front.

Die-cut four photo corners from red card stock; adhere photo corners to corners of black/white print paper on card.

Using red ink, stamp decorative heart on white card stock; use black ink to stamp 'love you!' on top of stamped heart. Cut a 2⅝ x 2⅝-inch square around stamped images; ink edges with brown ink. Adhere to red card stock; trim a narrow border. Wrap ribbon around bottom edge of stamped square; tie a knot on left side. Trim ends. Adhere assembled panel to card front.

Carefully take apart premade envelope and use as a template to trace and cut an envelope from white card stock; score and fold to form envelope flaps. Adhere side and bottom flaps together.

Use top envelope flap as a template to trace and cut a piece of black/white print paper to fit flap; adhere paper to top flap. ■

SOURCES: Printed paper from Carolee's Creations & Co.; rubber stamps from Paper Inspirations Inc. and My Sentiments Exactly!; die-cutting tool and die from QuicKutz Inc.

Crazy in Love

Love takes flight with a variety of embossing inks.

DESIGN BY CONNIE PETERTONJES

Materials

Card stock: black, red, white, red textured

Printed papers: red speckle, black-and-white newsprint, red-and-white script

Rubber stamps: Vaughn Font set, Spy Stencil Font set, Identity Femme set (includes wings and 'CRAZY')

Ink pads: charcoal chalk, clear distress embossing

Tattered Rose Distress embossing powder

Clear ultra-thick embossing enamel

Metallic rub-on creams: red, gray

Wooden fleur-de-lis

Paper flower

¼-inch-wide black-and-white gingham ribbon

Dot Fill template

Waxed paper

Light source such as a light box, window, etc.

Embossing stylus

Heat tool

Cotton balls

Removable tape

Adhesive dots

Paper glue

Form a 7 x 5-inch top-folded card from black card stock.

Cut two 3¼ x 2¼-inch rectangles from red card stock; cut rectangles the same size from red textured card stock and red speckle printed paper.

Place Dot Fill template face down on light source and secure with removable tape. Rub the backs of the red card-stock rectangles with waxed paper; this will allow embossing stylus to run smoothly around card stock. Place a red rectangle face down on template and emboss dot background onto rectangle; repeat for other red rectangle.

Dab a cotton ball into charcoal ink and rub ink onto two edges on each rectangle; rub the same ink across embossed rectangles. Referring to photo, adhere rectangles to card front with the inked edges along outer edges. The embossed rectangles are placed in the lower left and upper right corners.

Cut a 2 x 1½-inch rectangle from black-and-white newsprint printed paper; tear in half diagonally and ink edges with charcoal ink. Adhere torn pieces to lower left and upper right corners of card front.

Using provided pattern, trace and cut a heart from red-and-white script printed paper; ink edges with charcoal ink. Use the same ink and Vaughn Font alphabet stamps to stamp 'IN' on heart.

Use clear distress embossing ink to stamp two wings onto black card stock; emboss wings with Tattered Rose embossing powder. Once cool, rub finger over embossed images to give a distressed effect. Cut out embossed wings and adhere to heart, referring to photo for placement. Adhere heart and wings to card front.

Stamp 'CRAZY' on upper left corner of card with charcoal ink. Use Spy Stencil Font stamps and clear distress embossing ink to stamp 'LOVE' on white card stock; emboss word with clear embossing enamel. **Note:** *To prevent larger crystals from blowing off project before design is embossed, heat design from the back of the paper.*

Rub charcoal ink across top of embossed design with a cotton ball; rub a clean cotton ball over

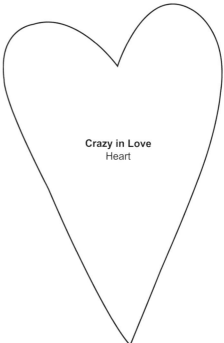

Crazy in Love
Heart

inked design to remove excess ink. Tear paper around edges of design; adhere to lower right corner of card.

Rub red metallic cream onto wooden fleur-de-lis; add a small amount of gray metallic cream as a highlighter. Tie flower onto fleur-de-lis with ribbon; adhere to lower left area of heart with adhesive dots. ■

SOURCES: Printed papers from 7gypsies, Keeping Memories Alive and Scenic Route Paper Co.; rubber stamps from Art Declassified; chalk ink pad from Clearsnap Inc.; embossing enamel, clear distress embossing ink pad and embossing powder from Ranger Industries Inc.; flower from Doodlebug Design Inc.; wooden fleur-de-lis from Darice Inc.; metallic rub-on creams from Craf-T Products; template from Lasting Impressions for Paper Inc.

Sending You My Love

Add a tag of love to a special valentine gift.

DESIGN BY KATHLEEN PANEITZ

Materials

Textured card stock: light blue, gray, pink, white
Printed mini pocket
Black dye ink pad
'adore' sticker
'always' mini tag
Heart stick pin
2 small heart coasters
Rub-on transfers: harlequin background,
    'love letters,' 'XO,' 'SWAK'
'Sending you my love' embellishment
⅝-inch-wide red dots grosgrain ribbon
Black dye ink pad
Paper adhesive

Cut a 4⅛ x 4½-inch rectangle from light blue card stock; cut off top corners diagonally, forming a tag. Ink edges.

Cut a 3⅜ x 4⅛-inch rectangle from gray card stock; apply harlequin background rub-on transfer to gray rectangle. Ink edges and adhere to tag ¼ inch from left edge.

Cut a piece of pink card stock to fit inside mini pocket; apply 'love letters' rub-on transfer to centre top of pink card stock. Insert piece inside mini pocket; adhere pocket to right side of tag.

Apply 'XO' rub-on transfers along left edge of tag; apply 'SWAK' rub-on transfer to lower right corner of tag.

Adhere 'sending you my love' embellishment to white card stock; trim a small border. Adhere to lower left area of tag, referring to photo for placement.

Adhere heart coasters to upper right corner of mini pocket on tag. Attach 'adore' sticker to tag to the left of mini pocket and above 'sending you my love' embellishment.

Fold ribbon in half and adhere to centre top of tag. Attach 'always' tag to ribbon with stick pin. ∎

SOURCES: Mini pocket from The Paper Loft; 'Sending you my love' embellishment from me & my BIG ideas; rub-on transfers from My Mind's Eye Inc. and 7gypsies; heart coasters from Imagination Project Inc./Gin-X; sticker and mini tag from Making Memories; stick pin from Heidi Grace Designs; ribbon from Pebbles Inc.; Paper-Tac adhesive from Beacon Adhesives Inc.

Easter Word Hunt

Let kids hunt Easter words before it's time for eggs.

DESIGN BY TAMI MAYBERRY

Materials
Card stock: lavender textured, cream, black
Scrap paper
Black round button
Small pencil
Black fine-tip marker (optional)
1¾ inches 1½-inch-wide ivory grosgrain ribbon
Flower foam stamp
Ivory acrylic paint
Foam brush
Craft knife
Tape
Adhesive dots and/or mounting squares
Computer and printer

Form a 5⅜ x 4¼-inch top-folded card from lavender textured card stock. Use ivory acrylic paint to stamp flowers randomly on front and back; let first side dry before moving to the other. Cut off bottom ½-inch on card front. Adhere button to a flower on left side of card.

To make word-search puzzle, first write the letters for the following words in a rectangular format on scrap paper: 'Easter,' 'Bunny,' 'Eggs,' 'Basket,' 'Bonnet' and 'Hunt.' Write various letters between these letters, creating a word-search puzzle. Use a computer to generate each line of letters; change the font of the letters to a typewriter style that will keep the text in a box format. Add a numbered list of the hidden words below puzzle. All text needs to fit within a 2⅝ x 3½-inch rectangle.

Print puzzle on cream card stock; cut out to size instructed above. **Option:** *Instead of using a computer, use black fine-tip marker to hand-write letters and words in a word-search puzzle format on cream card stock.*

Adhere puzzle to black card stock; trim a small border. Adhere to right side of card.

Use craft knife to cut a 1½-inch slit centred at the bottom back edge of card, just below the card front. Thread ribbon through slit, securing bottom end on reverse side of back with tape.

Cut a 5⅜ x 3¾-inch piece of cream card stock; adhere inside card, catching other end of ribbon, creating a loop. Make sure pencil fits inside loop.

Cut a 5⅜ x 1¾-inch piece of cream card stock; adhere to back of card, letting bottom edge extend beyond bottom of card. Insert pencil inside ribbon loop. ∎

SOURCES: Foam stamp from Making Memories.

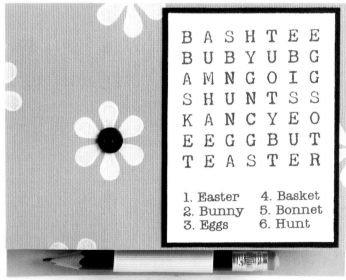

Ribbon Grass Easter

Pale green ribbon forms a grassy base for stamped Easter eggs.

DESIGN BY SHERRY WRIGHT

Materials

5½ x 4¼-inch green blank note card with envelope
Card stock: green, pink, blue
Egg rubber stamp
Brown dye ink pad
Coloured pencils
Ribbon: ³⁄₁₆-inch-wide light green grosgrain,
 ¼-inch-wide green grosgrain stitched,
 ⅛-inch-wide green stitched
Dies: alphabet, small flower
Die-cutting machine
Hot-glue gun with glue sticks
Paper adhesive

Cut 6-inch lengths of both green stitched ribbons; adhere ribbons to bottom of card, wrapping and adhering ends inside. Cut approximately fifteen 3-inch lengths of light green ribbon; knot the centre of each and hot-glue ribbon knots to bottom of card, allowing ribbons to overlap, forming the look of grass.

Die-cut 'Happy' from blue card stock and 'Easter' from pink card stock. Die-cut six small flowers from pink and blue card stocks; adhere 'Happy Easter' and flowers to card as shown.

Stamp nine eggs onto card stock, stamping four eggs on pink card stock, three eggs on blue and two eggs on green. Colour flowers on eggs with coloured pencils; cut out eggs. Set aside three eggs; adhere remaining six to card, nestling them underneath ribbon grass.

Cut a piece of green card stock to fit card front; adhere to reverse side, covering ribbon ends.

For envelope, adhere ⅛-inch-wide green stitched ribbon near bottom edge; trim edges even. Cut two 3-inch lengths of light green ribbon; knot the centre of each and adhere to lower right corner of envelope. Adhere remaining eggs to envelope as desired. ■

SOURCES: Card stock, note card, envelope and rubber stamp from Paper Salon Inc.; ribbons from Making Memories; die-cutting machine and dies from QuicKutz Inc.; paper adhesive from Beacon Adhesives Inc.

Easter Blessings

Stamped flowers, cut from card stock, add dimensional interest to an easy Easter card.

DESIGN BY MELANIE DOUTHIT

Materials
Card stock: pink, yellow, green
Printed papers: pink floral striped, blue floral
Pink envelope to fit a 5½ x 4¼-inch card
Easter sentiments: 'EASTER BLESSINGS,' Easter quotation
Rubber stamps: flowers, leaves
Dye ink pads: green, pink
Pink glimmer chalk
Adhesive foam squares
Glue stick

Form a 5½ x 4¼-inch top-folded card from pink card stock. Adhere a 5 x 3⅞-inch piece of blue floral paper to yellow card stock; trim a small border and adhere to card. Cut a 5-inch stripe from pink floral striped paper; adhere to card 1 inch from bottom.

Use both inks to stamp three leaves and five flowers on pink and green card stocks; cut out images. Cut a 1⅜-inch circle around 'EASTER BLESSINGS'; chalk surface of circle and adhere to centre of a pink flower. Adhere leaves and flowers to card as shown, using

foam squares for the flower with Easter greeting.

For inside of card, cut a 3½ x 2¼-inch rectangle around Easter quotation; chalk surface of rectangle. Adhere to yellow card stock; trim a small border and adhere again to blue floral printed paper. Trim a small border. Use both inks to stamp two flowers on green and pink card stocks; cut out flowers and adhere to upper left corner of quotation. Adhere assembled panel inside card.

Decorate envelope with printed papers as desired. ■

SOURCES: Printed papers, rubber stamps and ink pads from Paper Salon Inc.; Easter sentiments from Crossed Paths; glimmer chalk from Craf-T Products.

Some Bunny Loves You

Send Easter greetings with a touch of whimsy provided by our bunny.

DESIGN BY KATHLEEN PANEITZ

Materials
White card stock
Printed papers: Midnight Diamonds, Boy Zachary
Herbanella Easter border strip
Bunny page accent
Letter rub-on transfers
Sepia ink pad
Pink embroidery floss
Natural-colour scrapper's floss
Embroidery needle
Paper glue

Cut a 5½ x 8½-inch piece of white card stock; score and fold in half to make a 5½ x 4¼-inch card.

Cut a 5½ x 4¼-inch piece of diamonds printed paper; adhere to front of card. Adhere a 1-inch-wide strip of Zachary printed paper across bottom front of card, as shown.

Adhere border strip above Zachary paper. Cut the ears from the bunny page accent; adhere above border strip. Using pink floss and needle, stitch over stitching pattern on ears.

Ink edges of card front using sepia ink pad.

Tie a double strand of scrapper's floss around card front and knot in centre.

Use rub-on transfers to add 'SOME bunny Loves YOU' message over Zachary paper. ■

SOURCES: Printed paper from Bo-Bunny Press and BasicGrey; border strip and page accent from All My Memories; Portobello Road Letters and Lovey Dovey Fortunes rub-on transfers from 7gypsies; Center City Designs Tribeca Alphabet rub-on transfers from Imagination Project.

4U Mother

Create a card especially for mom using ribbons, printed paper and machine stitching.

DESIGN BY MELANIE DOUTHIT

Materials

Ivory card stock
Printed papers: yellow polka-dot, floral
Ivory envelope to fit a 5½ x 4¼-inch card
Alphabet stickers to spell 'MOM'
'MOTHER' chipboard rectangle
Brown chalk ink pad
Rub-on transfers: '4,' 'u'
Heart-shaped tag
Small light green safety pin
⅜-inch-wide sage green satin ribbon
Sewing machine with off-white thread
Adhesive foam tape
Paper adhesive

Form a 5½ x 4¼-inch top-folded card from ivory card stock; ink edges. Cut a 5½ x 2¾-inch piece of yellow polka-dot printed paper; ink edges and adhere to card. Cut a 5½ x 1½-inch piece of floral printed paper; ink edges and adhere to card as shown. Machine-stitch top and bottom edges of both rectangles.

Wrap ribbon through card and knot on front; trim ribbon ends. Apply rub-on transfers to heart tag; ink edges. Attach heart to ribbon knot with safety pin. Adhere heart to card with foam tape. Adhere 'MOTHER' chipboard rectangle to card as shown.

For envelope, cut a 5½ x 4⅛-inch piece of yellow polka-dot printed paper and a 5½ x 2¼-inch piece of floral printed paper; ink edges of both. Adhere floral piece to centre of yellow polka-dot piece; machine-stitch top and bottom edges of floral rectangle. Adhere rectangle to envelope. Attach alphabet stickers to envelope; ink edges of envelope. ■

SOURCES: Printed papers from Flair Designs and Scenic Route Paper Co.; stickers, heart-shaped tag and rub-on transfers from Flair Designs; chipboard rectangle from K&Company; chalk ink pad from Clearsnap Inc.

Thank You, Mom

Create a vintage look with distress inks and tea-dyed hues.

DESIGN BY VANESSA HUDSON

Materials

Printed papers: 3 patterns
Pale tan card stock
4⅛ x 9⅝-inch kraft envelope
Mini tan card-stock tag
Stickers
Alphabet rubber stamps
Brown ink pad
Brown distress ink
Antique heart charm

2 antique metal hinges
Antique mini brads
¾-inch-wide picot-edge ribbon
Fine string
¹⁄₁₆-inch circle punch
Craft knife
Sewing machine with dark red thread
Craft cement or adhesive dots
Paper glue or double-sided tape
Computer and printer

Project notes: *Give your project a vintage look by choosing papers and card stock in 'tea-dyed' hues, and by rubbing all edges and surfaces with distress ink.*

Adhere papers using paper glue or double-sided tape; use craft cement or adhesive dots for ribbons, string and charms.

Use computer to generate, or hand-print, lettering. Or, use alphabet stamps and a brown ink pad, or alphabet rub-on transfers.

Envelope: Cut printed papers in pieces to cover flap side of envelope, leaving narrow borders uncovered. Machine-stitch a 4¼ x 2¾-inch piece of printed paper to card stock, leaving ½-inch margin on left edge for hinge. Print 'MOM' on paper panel; tear down right edges.

Knot ribbon around 'MOM' cover. Print 'Thank you' on tiny card stock tag. Punch ¹⁄₁₆-inch hole through tag; tie to ribbon with string. Adhere sticker to back of 'MOM' cover. Attach cover to envelope using hinges and antique mini brads.

Print message on card stock; trim to measure 3¾ x 1¾ inches. Adhere to printed paper; trim, leaving narrow border. Adhere to envelope under 'MOM' cover.

Print 'to … from' information on printed paper; trim in label shape and adhere to reverse side of envelope. Embellish with stickers. Thread heart charm onto string; knot ribbon and adhere over string, at upper right corner of label.

Message strips: Cut card stock strips for messages to fit in envelope. Machine-stitch printed papers over ends; add stickers and desired messages. Insert strips in envelope. ■

Mother To Be

Celebrate Mother's Day with your favourite mom-to-be.

DESIGN BY SANDRA GRAHAM SMITH

Materials
Card stock: pink, white, black
Green polka-dot printed double-sided card stock
White envelope to fit a 5½ x 4¼-inch card
Rubber stamps: pregnant woman, mother definition
Black fine-detail pigment ink pad
Coloured pencils
⅛-inch-wide black polka-dot ribbon
Paper adhesive

Form a 5½ x 4¼-inch top-folded card from pink card stock. Adhere a 5½ x 2-inch piece of green polka-dot printed card stock to bottom half of card. Referring to photo, adhere ribbon along top edge of green polka-dot card stock; trim ribbon ends.

Stamp pregnant woman image on white card stock; colour. Cut a ⅞ x 3-inch rectangle around image and adhere to reverse side of green polka-dot card stock; trim a small border. Adhere to black card stock; trim a small border. Adhere ribbon to right edge of border; trim ribbon ends. Adhere to right side of card.

Stamp mother definition on white card stock; cut out image and colour as desired. Adhere to green polka-dot printed card stock. Trim a small border; adhere to black card stock and trim a small border. Adhere ribbon to left edge of border. Adhere to upper left corner of card.

Decorate envelope with green polka-dot printed card stock and ribbon. ◼

SOURCES: Mother definition rubber stamp from Oriental Trading Co.; ink pad from Tsukineko Inc.

Vintage Father's Day Card

Distressed paper gives you a head start on this weathered card.

DESIGN BY LISA JOHNSON

Materials
Card stock: olive green, burgundy, kraft
Red distressed printed paper
Kraft envelope to fit a 5½ x 4¼-inch card
Aged copper buckle
Rubber stamps: Father's Day sentiment, star, small decorative motif, 2 vintage labels, ticket
Brown pigment ink pad
Dye ink pads: brown, light brown, burgundy, olive green
Copper embossing powder
12½ inches 1½-inch-wide twill ribbon
Aged copper spiral clip
8 aged copper round mini brads
Bleach
Cotton swab
1⁄16-inch hole punch
Bone folder
Embossing heat tool
Mini adhesive dots
Permanent adhesive

Cut a 5½ x 8½-inch piece of olive green card stock; score and fold in half, forming a 5½ x 4¼-inch card. Cut a 5¼ x 4-inch piece of red distressed printed paper. Set aside.

Use brown dye ink to stamp star image onto burgundy card stock; lightly sprinkle copper embossing powder onto star and heat with embossing tool until powder is melted. Use cotton swab to apply bleach onto desired areas of star; let dry. Cut out star. Place star on upper right side of red distressed printed paper; punch a 1⁄16-inch hole through centre and insert a brad.

Stamp the following onto kraft card stock: small decorative motif and one vintage label with olive green ink, ticket with brown dye ink and remaining vintage label with burgundy ink. Cut out images. Use bone folder to roughen up the edges of stamped images. Ink edges with matching colour ink. Rub light brown ink on stamped images.

Use spiral clip to attach vintage labels together; use adhesive dots to adhere labels to upper left portion of red distressed printed paper. Adhere ticket to lower right corner.

Ink Father's Day sentiment with brown pigment ink and stamp onto twill ribbon approximately 2 inches from right end; heat set with heat tool. Age twill by dragging light brown ink pad across surface. Wrap twill around bottom portion of red distressed printed paper and wrap ends onto buckle, positioning sentiment on left side. Secure ends of twill by punching two 1⁄16-inch holes through each end and inserting brads. Fray ends of twill.

Place stamped decorative motif on lower left corner of red distressed printed paper; punch a 1⁄16-inch hole through centre and insert a brad. Centre and adhere assembled panel to card front.

For envelope, cut a 1½ x 4¾-inch piece of red distressed printed paper. Ink a vintage label image with olive green ink and stamp onto kraft card stock; cut out. Place image on bottom portion of red distressed printed paper and punch a 1⁄16-inch hole through each end. Insert brads. Adhere paper to left side of envelope. Rub light brown ink on envelope. ∎

SOURCES: Printed paper, rubber stamps, ink pads, metal embellishments and permanent adhesive from Stampin' Up!.

All Dad's Names

'Dad' means the same thing, no matter what language it's spoken in.

DESIGN BY TANIS GIESBRECHT

Materials

Card stock: blue, yellow
Father Words printed paper
Approximately 2-inch-square father/child photo
White envelope to fit a 5½ x 4¼-inch card
Black fine-tip marker
Grosgrain ribbon: 1-inch-wide multicoloured striped,
⅜-inch-wide olive green
Paper-piercing tool
Distressing tool
Stapler with staples
⅛-inch hole punch
Dimensional crystal lacquer
Paper adhesive
Computer and printer (optional)

Form a 5½ x 4¼-inch top-folded card from blue card stock. Adhere a 4⅛ x 4¼-inch piece of Father Words paper to left side of card, aligning edges. Adhere photo to a 2½-inch-square piece of blue card stock; distress edges. Cut two 2-inch pieces of multicoloured striped ribbon and one 3-inch

length of olive green ribbon; fold each in half and staple to left side of photo, tucking olive green ribbon inside one of the striped ribbons. Adhere photo to left side of card front.

Cut a ⅞ x 4¼-inch piece of yellow card stock; pierce holes along right edge. Distress edges and adhere to card as shown. Adhere a 4¼-inch length of olive green ribbon to yellow card stock. Punch twelve ⅛-inch circles from blue card stock; adhere circles, evenly spaced, to olive green ribbon on card. Apply a dot of crystal lacquer on top of each circle; let dry.

Cut a 5-inch length of multicoloured striped ribbon; trim ends in V-notches; adhere inside card. Hand-print, or use a computer to generate, 'He didn't tell me how to live; he lived, and let me watch him do it. Clarence Budington Kelland' and 'Happy Father's Day' on yellow card stock, leaving space between quotation and author. Cut a rectangle around words; distress edges. Adhere inside card, overlapping ribbon.

Decorate envelope with Father Words paper and ribbon as desired. ■

SOURCES: Printed paper from Flair Designs; distressing tool from Heidi Swapp/Advantus Corp.; paper-piercing tool from Making Memories; Crystal Effects lacquer from Stampin' Up!

My Role Model

Tell dad what he really means to you with an easy card featuring rub-on transfers.

DESIGN BY MARY AYRES

Materials
Light brown card stock
Assorted printed papers
White vellum
White envelope to fit a 5 x 7-inch card
Rub-on transfers: 'my Father,' assorted dad-
    themed words
Brown dye ink pad
12 pewter mini square brads
1/16-inch hole punch
Sewing machine with metallic gold thread
Instant-dry paper glue

Cut a 10 x 7-inch piece of light brown card stock; score and fold in half, forming a 5 x 7-inch card. Ink edges. Machine-stitch along edges on card front.

Cut the following rectangles from assorted printed papers: three 2½ x 1½-inch, two 1¾ x 1½-inch and one 1¾ x 2-inch. Ink edges of each.

Referring to photo, adhere rectangles to card front. Machine-stitch along edges of the three smaller rectangles on card front. Transfer a dad-themed word onto each smaller rectangle.

Tear three 2 x 1-inch rectangles from vellum; ink edges. Transfer a dad-themed word onto each vellum rectangle. Place vellum rectangles on remaining larger rectangles; punch 1/16-inch holes through vellum corners. Attach brads, securing vellum in place. Transfer 'my Father' to lower portion of card front.

For envelope, ink front edges. Cut a 2⅝-inch-wide strip of printed paper to fit along left side of envelope front. Ink edges of printed paper. Machine-stitch along edges of printed paper. Transfer a dad-themed word onto printed paper. Adhere paper to left side of envelope front. ■

SOURCES: Printed papers from K&Company; rub-on transfers from Royal & Langnickel; paper glue from Beacon Adhesives Inc.

Pumpkin, Treats & Fun

Send brightly coloured Halloween wishes to your favourite ghosties and ghoulies.

DESIGN BY SUSAN STRINGFELLOW

Materials
Black library pocket
Multicoloured 'Halloween' polka-dot printed
   paper
3 Halloween-themed word charms
Alphabet rubber stamps
Black dye ink pad
Black craft wire
⅛-inch dowel rod
8 flower sequins
Bat button
Seed beads: 3 clear, 8 orange
White acrylic paint
⅜-inch-wide ribbon: yellow, orange, purple
Nylon beading thread
Beading needle
Sewing machine with black thread
Paintbrush
⅛-inch hole punch
Wire nippers
Glue stick

Carefully take apart library pocket. Cut a 3½ x 1-inch piece of polka-dot printed paper including 'Halloween' along bottom edge; adhere paper to the front of the pocket 1⅛ inch above bottom edge. Machine-stitch along edges of polka-dot paper.

Use beading thread and beading needle to hand-sew a flower sequin to lower right corner on pocket front; stitch an orange seed bead onto flower centre, securing flower to pocket. Repeat four additional times.

Wrap black wire around dowel rod for approximately 3½ inches, creating a coil; remove coil from rod. Paint the back of each word charm white; let dry. String a 1-inch length of wire through each charm and attach to wire coil, wrapping wire ends around each other to secure. Reassemble library pocket and punch a ⅛-inch hole through upper sides of pocket front and back; thread wire ends through holes and wrap wires around themselves to secure. Trim excess wire if needed.

Cut a 3 x 4½-inch rectangle from green card stock. Cut a 1 x 4½-inch piece of polka-dot printed paper and adhere to green rectangle ⅜ inch from left edge. Cut a 4½-inch length of orange ribbon and adhere to left edge of polka-dot printed rectangle.

Cut a 2-inch length of each colour of ribbon; fold each in half and machine-stitch them to upper left edge of green rectangle. Continue to machine-stitch along perimeter of rectangle and along right edge of polka-dot printed paper. In the same manner as for library pocket, hand-sew three flower sequins and seed beads to upper right corner. Hand-sew bat button to upper left corner, threading three clear seed beads on top of bat. Using alphabet rubber stamps and black ink, stamp 'happy halloween!' on rectangle. Insert rectangle inside library pocket. ■

SOURCES: Library pocket from Bazzill Basics; printed paper, word charms, button and flower sequins from Doodlebug Design Inc.; wire from Artistic Wire; rubber stamps from EK Success; pearlescent ink pad from Jacquard Products.

happy halloween!

treats fun pumpkin

halloween

Spooky, Creepy Tags & Card

Re-create the excitement of Halloween with amusing papers and images.

DESIGNS BY HEIDI LARSEN

Materials

Card stock: pale green, black, purple
Halloween-themed stickers, including a moon and twill alphabet
'halloween' rub-on transfer
Ink pads: brown, white
Assorted orange, black and gold ribbons
Gold rickrack
Assorted brads, including 3 large
Hole punches: 1/16- and 1/8-inch

Tags: Cut three 3 x 5⅛-inch rectangles from card stock; trim top corners diagonally, forming tags. Ink edges with contrasting colours of inks. Decorate bottom portions of tags with stickers. If desired, attach a large sticker to card stock; trim a narrow border; ink edges and adhere to tag(s). Accent tags with ribbons and brads as desired.

Cut three 1 x 1⅝-inch rectangles from contrasting colours of card stock; ink edges with contrasting colours of inks and attach to centre tops of tags with large brads. If desired, wrap small pieces of ribbon around rectangles.

Card: Cut a 4 x 12-inch piece of black card stock; score and fold in half, forming a 4 x 6-inch top-folded card. Attach a moon sticker to lower left area of card front. Apply 'halloween' rub-on transfer along right side of card front, overlapping sticker.

Attach twill alphabet stickers to top of card to spell 'happy.' Punch a 1/16-inch hole at each end of

'happy' and insert brads.

Punch three 1/8-inch holes through lower left side of card front; tie rickrack through each hole and double knot; trim rickrack ends. Ink card edges with white ink.

Tie orange ribbon through top of card and tie a knot on right side; trim ribbon ends. Tie black and gold ribbons next to knot; trim ribbon ends. ■

SOURCES: Stickers, rub-on transfer, chocolate paper stain ink and brads from All My Memories; vintage wine and light earth green card stock from Bazzill Basics; Fresco white ink from Gary M. Burlin.

Magic Potions

Conjure your creative magic for this little charmer filled with note cards.

DESIGN BY SUSAN HUBER

Materials
Metal tin
Card stock: black, green, yellow, orange
Vintage Halloween-themed images
Alphabet rub-on transfers
Brown dye ink pad
Small Halloween-themed buttons
Co-ordinating fibres
Green piping cord
Sandpaper
Rounded corner punch
Clear spray sealer (optional)
Double-sided tape
Adhesive foam tape

Cut out vintage image; round corners with punch and adhere to black card stock. Trim a narrow border and round corners with punch. Lightly sand image. Wrap fibres around image and tie a knot; trim fibre ends. Use double-sided tape to adhere image to top of tin lid. Adhere a few buttons to lid as desired. Wrap and adhere piping cord to edge of tin lid.

Cut a piece of green card stock to fit inside tin lid; ink as desired. Cut out a vintage image and adhere to top of card stock with foam tape. Wrap a fibre around upper right corner of image. Apply alphabet rub-on transfers below image to spell 'Magic Potions.' Adhere a button below words. Adhere inside tin lid.

Cut five 4 x 3⅜-inch rectangles from card stock; score and fold each in half, forming 2 x 3⅜-inch cards. Round corners with punch. Ink edges. Cut out vintage images to fit on card fronts. Adhere desired images to card stock with foam tape and trim narrow borders. Ink edges. Adhere layered images to card fronts. Wrap a piece of fibre around each card front and tie knots; trim fibre ends. Adhere buttons to card fronts. Place cards inside tin.

Cut a piece of card stock to fit bottom of tin; round the corners with punch and ink edges. Adhere card stock to bottom of tin. If desired, open tin and spray sealer on top of box lid only; leave tin open while sealer dries. ■

SOURCES: Vintage images from Altered Pages; rub-on transfers from Doodlebug Design Inc.; distress ink pad from Ranger Industries; buttons from Jesse James & Co.

Joyeux Noel

Sandpaper provides just the right amount of distressing on this easy Christmas card.

DESIGN BY SUSAN STRINGFELLOW

Materials
Card stock: black, white
Adhesive-backed card stock with white cores:
   white, pink, green, light green, red
Black alphabet stickers
3-inch-square black netting
Black fine-tip marker
Sandpaper
3 clear rhinestone brads
Punches: flower, ⅜-inch circle, ⅛-inch hole
Sewing machine with black thread
Paper adhesive

Form a 5½ x 4¼-inch top-folded card from black card stock. Cut a 5¼ x 4-inch rectangle from white adhesive-backed card stock. Punch seven flowers from pink card stock, nine flowers from green card stock, 11 flowers from light green card stock and 12 flowers from red card stock. Sand all flowers to reveal some of the white core; peel off backings and attach to white rectangle as shown. Trim edges. Attach rectangle to card front.

Machine-stitch along rectangle edges.

Punch six flowers from white card stock. Punch three ⅜-inch circles from red card stock. Use black marker to draw swirls on flower petals of three white flowers.

Place black netting on upper left corner of card front. Referring to photo, layer a red circle on top of a swirled flower and a solid white flower. Secure to card with a brad. Repeat to attach two additional flowers to card. Attach stickers to lower right area of card to spell 'JOYEUX NOEL.' ∎

SOURCES: Adhesive-backed card stock and stickers from Die Cuts With A View; flower and circle punches from EK Success; rhinestone brads from Making Memories.

Christmas Peace

Non-traditional colours and machine-stitching create a lovely handmade Christmas greeting.

DESIGN BY SUSAN STRINGFELLOW

Materials
Olive green card stock
Green/red/white striped paper
Co-ordinating tab
Co-ordinating paisley printed border sticker
Ivory envelope to fit a 4¼ x 5½-inch card
'peace' circle cutout
4¾ inches ⅜-burgundy velvet ribbon
Heart stick pin
Paper flower
Rubber stamps: reindeer, 'To:,' 'From:'
Black pigment ink pad
Clear embossing powder
Embossing heat tool
Sewing machine with burgundy thread
Double-sided tape
Glue stick

Form a 4¼ x 5½-inch card from olive green card stock. Cut a 3 x 5-inch rectangle from striped paper; adhere tab to lower right corner; adhere rectangle to left side of card front.

Stamp reindeer on lower right side of rectangle; stamp 'To:' and 'From:' on tab. Emboss all images with clear embossing powder. Machine-sew along edges of rectangle with a decorative stitch.

Adhere 'peace' cutout to card as shown; machine-stitch around edge. Adhere ribbon to card as shown. Adhere heart pin and flower to ribbon on card with double-sided tape.

For envelope, attach border sticker to top envelope flap; trim ends even. Machine-stitch along bottom edge with a decorative stitch. Stamp 'To:' and 'From:' on front of envelope. ∎

SOURCES: Printed paper, sticker, tab, cutout and flower from My Mind's Eye; rubber stamps from Stampin' Up!; heart pin from Nunn Design.

Embossed Joy

Sanding an embossed design allows the card stock's white core to show through.

DESIGN BY SUSAN STRINGFELLOW

Materials
Card stock with white cores: green, red
Printed papers: green polka-dot, Christmas-
    themed quotations
Waxed paper
3½ inches white pompom trim
2 mini candy canes*
Clear mini plastic ball pin*
White mini safety pin
Small beads to fit on safety pin: 1 red, 1 green
Sandpaper
Light source such as a light table, window, etc.
'joy' embossing template
Embossing stylus
Sewing machine with white thread
Tape
Paper glue

*These items should be available from your local craft store.

Form a 5-inch-square, top-folded card from green card stock; lightly sand edges. Cut a 4½-inch-square piece from green polka-dot printed paper; centre and adhere to card front.

Rub waxed paper over red card stock to help stylus glide smoothly. Place embossing template facedown on light source; secure with tape. Place red card stock facedown on template and use stylus to outline the design. Sand surface of embossed design; cut a 3½-inch square around embossed design. Centre and adhere to card. Adhere white pompom trim to bottom edge of embossed design.

Cut out a quotation from printed paper, cutting it into several rectangles; adhere rectangles along top and right edges of card. Machine-sew a zigzag stitch along edges of printed paper on card; straight stitch along edge of embossed design.

Attach mini candy canes and plastic ball pin to card by inserting them through left end of pompom trim; secure with a small amount of glue. Let dry. Slide beads onto safety pin; attach to pompom trim next to candy canes and plastic ball pin. ■

SOURCES: Card stock and printed papers from Die Cuts With A View; embossing template from Plaid Enterprises; mini safety pin from Making Memories.

Holly Spirals

Quilling lends a distinguished air to a gently weathered Christmas card.

DESIGN BY KATHLEEN PANEITZ

Materials
Card stock: white, green, dark red
Printed papers: aged barn red, buttercream script
Red alphabet stickers
Rubber stamps: holly berry border, music staffs collage
Black dye ink pad
Dark red fine-tip marker
Twill tape
Dark red raffia
Sandpaper
ENV-1 envelope template or template from page 154
Quilling tool
Mini adhesive dots
Paper adhesive
Computer and printer (optional)

Form a 5 x 4-inch top-folded card from white card stock; adhere a 5 x 4-inch piece of aged barn red paper to card. Sand edges.

Hand-print with dark red marker, or use a computer to generate, 'deck the halls with boughs of' on buttercream script paper. Cut a 4¼ x 3½-inch rectangle around words, positioning words along left edge; ink edges. Stamp music collage on upper right corner of buttercream rectangle; stamp holly berry border onto a 4½-inch length of twill tape; wrap twill around left side of rectangle, securing ends to reverse side with adhesive dots. Adhere assembled panel to card.

Colour berries on twill with dark red marker. Attach alphabet stickers to bottom edge of pale yellow rectangle to spell 'Holly.'

Cut four ⅛-inch-wide strips of green card stock and three ⅛-inch-wide strips of dark red card stock. Using quilling tool and referring to provided patterns, quill two green strips into marquise shapes and the two remaining green strips into leaf shapes; quill dark red strips into circles as holly berries. Use mini adhesive dots to hold ends of quilled shapes together; adhere to card as shown.

Tie a bow with raffia; adhere to upper left corner.

Form envelope from purchased template or template from page 154. Stamp music collage on lower left corner. ■

SOURCES: Printed papers from Scissor Sisters Inc.; stickers from Creative Imaginations; rubber stamps from Plaid Enterprises/All Night Media; envelope template from The C-Thru Ruler Co.

Holly Spirals
Circle

Holly Spirals
Marquise

Holly Spirals
Leaf

deck the halls with boughs of

HOLLY

Simple Card Set

Make dozens of these easy cards in an evening for all of your holiday needs.

DESIGN BY JEANNE WYNHOFF

Materials
Light sage green card stock
Printed paper: burgundy/green striped double-sided
Co-ordinating stickers: 4 holly leaves, 2 styles of Christmas trees, 'Noel' star, 'Noel' present
Metal 'Merry Christmas' tags
3/8-inch-wide green grosgrain ribbon
4 burgundy mini round brads
Envelopes to fit a 4¼-inch-square card
1/16-inch hole punch
Adhesive dots
Glue stick

Cut a 4¼ x 8½-inch piece of light sage green card stock; score and fold in half, forming a 4¼-inch square card. Determine if a top fold or a side fold card is desired. Cut a piece of striped paper to fit on card front; glue to card.

Cut a piece of ribbon long enough to wrap across width of card or height of card; using adhesive dots, attach ribbon to card, wrapping and adhering ends inside card. Trim ends.

Using an adhesive dot, attach a holly leaf sticker to the reverse side of a metal tag. Punch a 1/16-inch hole through ribbon as desired; insert a brad through metal tag and punched hole, securing tag to card. Attach Christmas sticker to card as desired.

For envelope, use template to trace and cut an envelope from striped paper; score and fold on lines to form envelope flaps. Glue side and bottom flaps together. ■

SOURCES: Printed paper from Keeping Memories Alive; stickers from O' Scrap; metal tags from Eyelet Outlet; Coluzzle template from Provo Craft.

Elegant Poinsettias

Embossed poinsettia cut-outs add dimension to your holiday greetings.

DESIGN BY SUSAN HUBER

Materials

Card stock: desired colours, including gray
Rubber stamps: Christmas frames within frame, large and small poinsettias
Watermark ink pad
Assorted pigment powders
Gum arabic powder
Gold embossing powder
Gold leafing pen
Gold mini round brads
Envelope template from page 155
Embossing heat tool
Paintbrush
1/16-inch hole punch
Craft knife
Gold glitter glue
Foam tape
Paper adhesive

Form a 5-inch-square card from desired card stock. Edge all edges with gold leafing pen. Set aside.

Stamp Christmas frame onto card stock; sprinkle image with gold embossing powder and emboss. Stamp and emboss three to five small and/or large poinsettias on card stock.

To colour frames and poinsettias, mix desired colours of pigments powders, gum arabic powder and water together until the mixture is of watercolour consistency. Paint embossed images; let dry.

Cut out each poinsettia, being careful to not cut through embossed outline. Punch a 1/16-inch hole through the centre of each poinsettia; insert brads.

Note: Do not bend prongs yet. Set poinsettias aside.

Using a craft knife, cut apart frames. If desired, layer largest frame on a different-colour card stock; edge with gold leafing pen. Arrange frames on card front as desired, adhering one or two with paper adhesive and adhering remaining frame(s) with foam tape.

Attach poinsettias to card as desired by punching a 1/16-inch hole through card stock and inserting brad already attached to poinsettia. Tuck some of the petals underneath frames. Curl petals by rolling them over a small paintbrush. If desired, a small piece of foam tape under each petal can be used to help hold the shape.

For bifold card, cut a 10 x 5-inch piece of card stock; score and fold vertical lines 2½ inches from left edge and 2½ inches from right edge. Edge all edges with gold leafing pen. Set aside

Stamp Christmas frame in same manner as before, along with a small poinsettia. Emboss and colour images in same manner as before. Let dry. Cut apart frames and cut out poinsettia, inserting a brad as before.

Adhere the largest frame to the left front card panel only, adhere the middle frame to the right front panel only, lining it up so it fits inside large frame. Punch a 1/16-inch hole through centre of remaining frame and insert brad of poinsettia. Adhere this frame to the left front card panel, positioning it so it fits in centre.

Form envelopes from co-ordinating card stock using template on page 155. Stamp one large and two small poinsettias on lower left corner of envelope front; sprinkle flowers with gold embossing powder

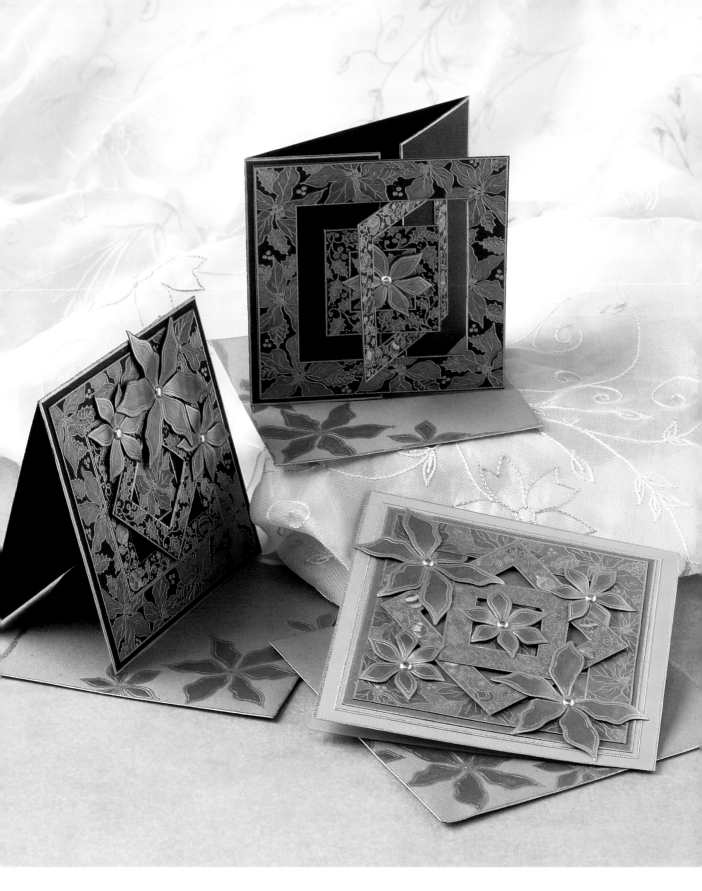

and emboss. Ink edges of envelope; sprinkle with embossing powder and emboss. Paint poinsettias in same manner as for cards. Apply a small amount of glitter glue to the centre of each. Let dry. ■

SOURCES: Rubber stamps from Magenta; ink pad from Tsukineko Inc; pigment powders from Jacquard Products; gold leafing pen from Krylon; envelope template from Stamp Your Art Out!

Metric Equivalency Chart

MM = Millimetres   CM = Centimetres

Inches to Millimetres and Centimetres

INCHES	MM	CM	INCHES	CM	INCHES	CM
⅛	3	0.3	9	22.9	30	76.2
¼	6	0.6	10	25.4	31	78.7
⅜	10	1.0	11	27.9	32	81.3
½	13	1.3	12	30.5	33	83.8
⅝	16	1.6	13	33.0	34	86.4
¾	19	1.9	14	35.6	35	88.9
⅞	22	2.2	15	38.1	36	91.4
1	25	2.5	16	40.6	37	94.0
1¼	32	3.2	17	43.2	38	96.5
1½	38	3.8	18	45.7	39	99.1
1¾	44	4.4	19	48.3	40	101.6
2	51	5.1	20	50.8	41	104.1
2½	64	6.4	21	53.3	42	106.7
3	76	7.6	22	55.9	43	109.2
3½	89	8.9	23	58.4	44	111.8
4	102	10.2	24	61.0	45	114.3
4½	114	11.4	25	63.5	46	116.8
5	127	12.7	26	66.0	47	119.4
6	152	15.2	27	68.6	48	121.9
7	178	17.8	28	71.1	49	124.5
8	203	20.3	29	73.7	50	127.0

Baby Tag Cards TEMPLATE FROM PAGE 82

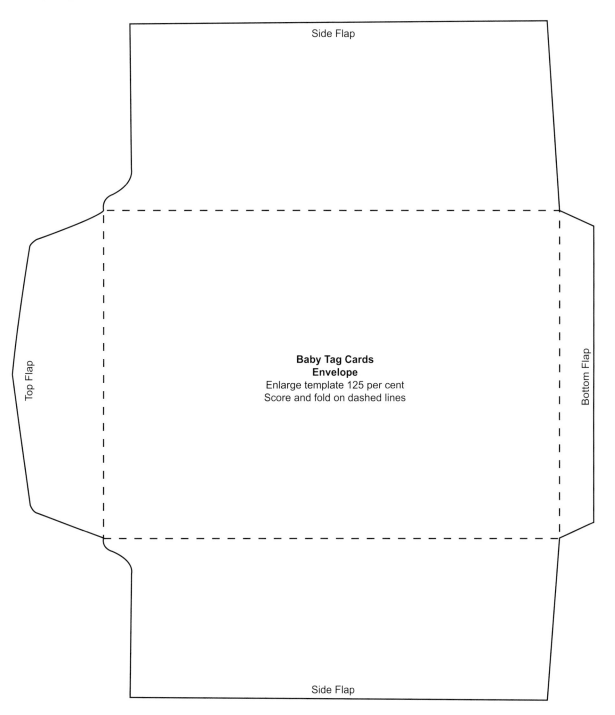

Side Flap

Top Flap

Baby Tag Cards
Envelope
Enlarge template 125 per cent
Score and fold on dashed lines

Bottom Flap

Side Flap

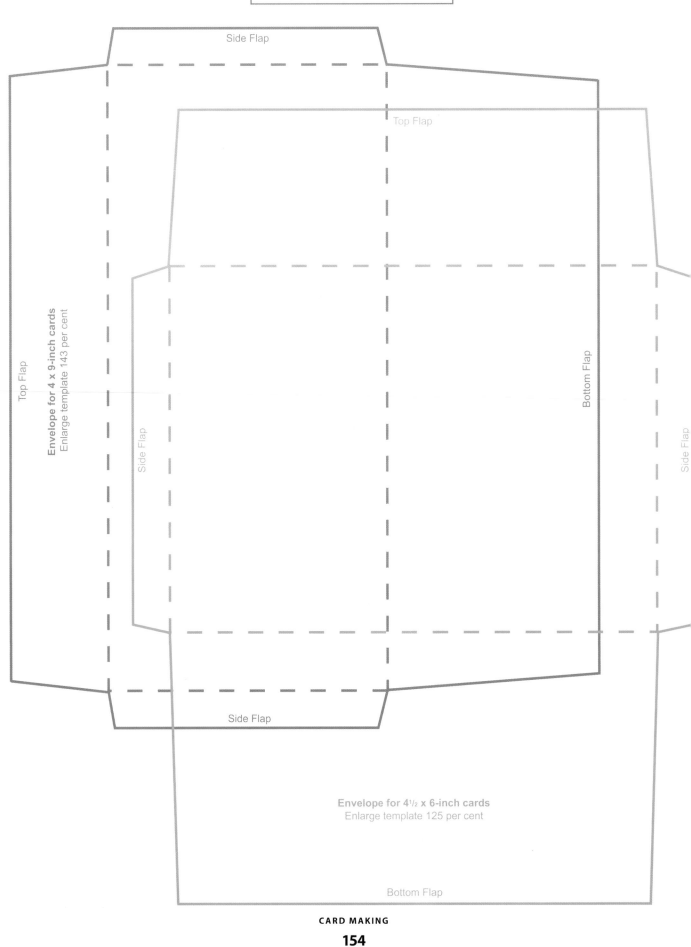

Side Flap

Top Flap

Envelope for 4 x 9-inch cards
Enlarge template 143 per cent

Top Flap

Bottom Flap

Side Flap

Side Flap

Side Flap

Side Flap

Envelope for 4¹/₂ x 6-inch cards
Enlarge template 125 per cent

Bottom Flap

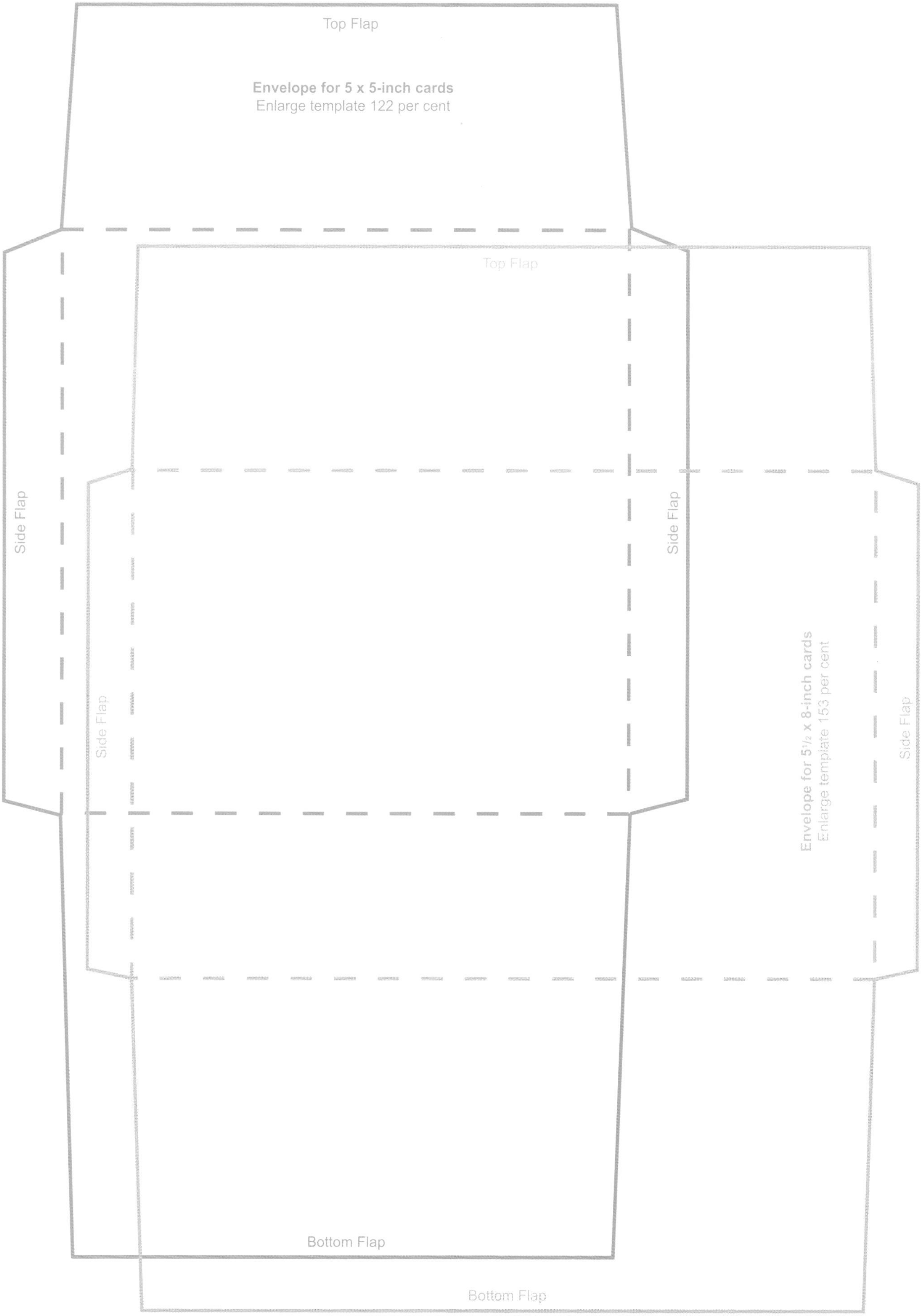

Top Flap

Envelope for 5 x 5-inch cards
Enlarge template 122 per cent

Top Flap

Side Flap

Side Flap

Side Flap

Side Flap

Envelope for 5½ x 8-inch cards
Enlarge template 153 per cent

Bottom Flap

Bottom Flap

INDEX

INDEX

INDEX

Our website is stuffed with all kinds of great information

www.companyscoming.com

Save up to 75% on cookbooks

Free recipes and cooking tips

Free newsletter with exclusive offers

Preview new titles

Find older titles no longer in stores

We have a sweet line up of cookbooks with plenty more in the oven

More than 25 years and more than 25 million cookbooks sold–that's quite a feat.
Now we're giving you the same attention to detail in our new craft books as we always
have in our cookbooks–lots of great photos, easy-to-follow instructions and choices galore!
It's time to get a little crafty with us!